A HISTORY OF
MULTICULTURAL AMERICA

The Great Migrations
1880s-1912

William Loren Katz

RSVP
**RAINTREE
STECK-VAUGHN**
PUBLISHERS
The Steck-Vaughn Company

Austin, Texas

For Laurie

Cover and interior design: Joyce Spicer
Electronic Production: Scott Melcer

Library of Congress Cataloging-in-Publication Data

Katz, William Loren.
    The great migrations, 1880s-1912 / by William Loren Katz.
      p.   cm. — (A history of multicultural America)
    Includes index.
    Summary: Describes the massive wave of immigration experienced by the United States between 1880 and World War I and the experiences of the immigrants from Europe, the Middle East, and Asia.
    ISBN 0-8114-6278-1   ISBN 0-8114-2915-6 (soft cover)
    1. Minorities — United States — History — Juvenile literature.
2. Immigrants — United States — History — Juvenile literature.
3. United States — Emigration and immigration — History —
Juvenile literature. [1. Minorities — History. 2. Immigrants —
History. 3. United States — Emigration and immigration —
History.] I. Title. II. Series: Katz, William Loren. History of
multicultural America.
E184.A1K298   1993
973'.04—dc20   92-22426
                                          CIP
                                          AC

Printed and bound in the United States of America

1 2 3 4 5 6 7 8 9 0 LB 98 97 96 95 94 93

Acknowledgments

All prints and photos from the collection of the author, William L. Katz.

Cover Photographs: (inset) The Granger Collection; (map) North Wind Picture Archive

TABLE OF CONTENTS

INTRODUCTION

The history of the United States is the story of people of many backgrounds. A few became wealthy through their knowledge of science, industry, or banking. But it was ordinary people who most shaped the progress of this country and created our national heritage.

The American experience, however, has often been recounted in history books as the saga of powerful men—presidents and senators, merchants and industrialists. Schoolchildren were taught that the wisdom and patriotism of an elite created democracy and prosperity.

A truthful history of the United States has to do more than celebrate the contributions of the few. Ordinary Americans fought the Revolution that set this country free, and ordinary workers built the nation's economy. The overwhelming majority of people held no office, made little money, and worked hard all their lives.

Some groups, women and minorities in particular, had to vault legal barriers and public hostility in order to make their contributions to the American dream, only to find that school courses taught little about their achievements. The valiant struggle of minorities and women to win dignity, equality, and justice often was omitted from history's account. Some believe this omission was accidental or careless; others insist it was purposeful.

Native Americans struggled valiantly to survive military and cultural assaults on their lives. But the public was told Native Americans were savages undeserving of any rights to their land or culture. African Americans battled to break the chains of slavery and to scale the walls of racial discrimination. But a century after slavery ended, some textbooks still pictured African Americans as content under slavery and bewildered by freedom. Arrivals from Asia, Mexico, and the West Indies faced legal restrictions and sometimes violence. But the public was told that they were undeserving of a welcome because they took "American jobs," and some were "treacherous aliens."

Whether single, married, or mothers, women were portrayed as dependent on men and accepting of a lowly status. The record of their sturdy labors, enduring strengths, and their arduous struggle to achieve equality rarely found its way into classrooms. The version of American history that reached the public carried many prejudices. It often preferred farmers over urban workers, middle classes over working classes, rich over poor. Women and minorities became invisible, ineffective, or voiceless.

This distorted legacy also failed to mention the campaigns waged by minorities and women to attain human rights. Such efforts did not reflect glory on white male rulers and their unwillingness to extend democracy and opportunity to others.

This kind of history was not a trustworthy tale. It locked out entire races and impeded racial understanding. Not only was it unreliable, but for most students it was dull and boring.

Our history has to be truthful and complete. Our struggle to overcome the barriers of nature and obstacles made by humans is an inspiring story. This series of books seeks to explore the heroic efforts of minorities and women to find their place in the American dream.

William Loren Katz

CHAPTER 1

THE NEW IMMIGRATION

In 1886 the statue of "Liberty Enlightening the World," a gift from the people of France, was dedicated by President Grover Cleveland. Set at the entrance to New York Harbor, the statue was just in time to greet the biggest migration in global history.

Millions of people left Europe, the Middle East, and Asia for the United States. In the 1880s more people landed on American soil than in the thirty years before the Civil War.

Most European immigrants made the two-week trip in third-class quarters or steerage (the cheapest and most crowded spaces below deck). Morris Cohen, who later became a famous philosopher and writer, was packed with his family in steerage. "We were huddled together in the steerage literally like cattle — my mother, my sister, and I sleeping on the middle tier, people being above and below us." One women recalled, "The ship heaved and turned. People threw up, dishes fell, women screamed."

Between 1880 and World War I, about 22 million men, women, and children entered the United States. More than a million arrived in each of the years 1905, 1906, 1907, 1910, 1913, and 1914.

Emma Lazarus, born to Jewish immigrants in 1849, wrote the poem that appears on the Statue of Liberty: "...Give me your tired, your poor, Your huddled masses yearning to breathe free..."

By the early 20th century, travel to America was cheap and fast. The journey took one to two weeks. Steerage cost those leaving England $15, or a few dollars more from the European continent. Conditions were terrible. A 1910 U.S. government report cites "filth and stench" everywhere and called steerage accommodations "almost unendurable." A U.S. Immigration Service investigator who crossed the Atlantic disguised as a Bohemian peasant reported:

Everything was dirty, sticky, and disagreeable to the touch. Every impression was offensive.

Not everyone had to travel in steerage. Passengers who could afford the expense paid for first- or second-class quarters. Upon arrival these immigrants were examined by courteous officials who boarded the ships at anchor. But those in steerage were sent to a holding center for a full physical and mental examination. The facility at Ellis Island which opened in 1892 could process up to 5,000 people a day. On some days between 1905 and 1914 it had to process more than 10,000 immigrants a day.

But on the day they landed in 1906, Marie Prisland and 100 other Slovenian women found Ellis Island an exhilarating experience. A guard brought them a pail of water but some Slovenian men stepped forward first. The guard firmly pushed them back saying, "Ladies first." The women were shocked, Prisland said, because:

> . . . in Slovenia, as in all of Europe, women were always second to men. Someone dramatically explained it this way: "First comes man, then a long time nothing, then comes the woman."

> Happy at the sudden turn of events, one elderly lady stepped forward, holding a dipper of water and proposed this toast: "Long Live America, where women are first!"

Steerage was the lot of most of the "new immigrants." The trip in steerage took a fearful toll in lives lost and illness.

Ports of Entry

From 1855 until 1892, 8 million immigrants landed at Castle Garden in New York Harbor. Once a fancy theater for the wealthy, Castle Garden had been transformed into an immigrant center with plain wooden benches and bathroom stalls to receive millions of immigrants.

Facilities at Castle Garden, strained in the 1880s by huge numbers of arrivals, began to break down. Congressional investigators found shocking conditions. Arrivals were slipping through illegally. People had to sleep on floors or benches. Castle Garden was finally closed in 1890 to make way for Ellis Island.

New York was not the only port of entry. From 1846 to 1915, many Europeans entered the United States at Galveston, Texas. Promoted by Rabbi Henry Cohen and the large Jewish American community, Galveston called itself the gateway to the Midwest. It proved second to New York in its ability to attract immigrants. ■

Unlike previous immigrants, most newcomers between 1880 and 1914 were not from western Europe but from eastern and southern Europe. Italy sent more than 4 million immigrants to the United States, and Jews from eastern Europe numbered 2 million.

Many arrivals had left their homelands to escape mobs who attacked them because of their ethnicity, religion, or politics. The German, Russian, Austro-Hungarian, and Ottoman (Turkish) empires ruled over many different peoples and nationalities and often cruelly mistreated them.

Until 1899, U.S. immigration officials asked arrivals which nation they had left, not their religion or ancestry. So oppressed people were listed under the countries from which they fled. Armenians who escaped from Turkey were recorded as Turks, and Jews who had been beaten by mobs in Russia were listed as Russians.

The registry desk at Ellis Island.

Many people were lured to the United States by contractors sent by American corporations to hire cheap labor for their mines and mills. In 1883 a labor paper reported how these contractors recruited European workers from "some of the most wretched districts of Hungary, Italy, or Denmark" with "stories of fabulous wages . . . in America."

[The contractors] bamboozle the poor creatures, rope them in and make contracts with them to pay their passage that few can understand. When they reach the districts of this country to which the contractors ship them, they find their golden dreams turn into nightmares, as they are put to work in mines, factories, or on railroads, at even lower wages than those whom they threw out of work.

This so called "new immigration" was different in many other ways from previous immigration. For the first time, Catholic and Jewish immigrants outnumbered Protestants, and still other arrivals were Muslims, Buddhists, or Greek or Russian Orthodox church members.

Until 1870, 90 percent of all overseas immigrants had come from Protestant northern and western Europe. Many of these nations had

Immigrants waiting for the ferry to Manhattan from Ellis Island.

democratic traditions and education systems. Even among the poor, many had spent a few years in school or had acquired some industrial skills on the job, and more than a few spoke English. Many of these men and women settled in agricultural regions of the United States. Their goal was to buy readily available land and start small family farms.

On the other hand, the new immigrants left eastern and southern Europe from nations that did not have well-developed education systems nor did these nations allow ordinary citizens to vote. The newcomers also landed in a changed America, one that was turning away from agriculture to become a modern industrialized nation. For the most part, cheap land was no longer available.

These immigrants arrived without the money to buy farms in America, and they rejected work on such isolated places so distant from friends and relatives. They wanted to try urban life so they could live close to relatives and friends as they had in the "old country."

For this reason, they were willing to take jobs in mines and factories and endure crowded quarters. More than three fourths settled

A newly arrived family from Italy.

in large cities and in neighborhoods with relatives and friends. "All my relatives and all our neighbors — in fact, everybody who was anybody," wrote Marcus Ravage of his village of Vaslui, Romania, "had either gone or was going to New York."

The people of the new immigration differed from earlier arrivals in other ways. Very few spoke English, and some could not read or write any language. Most were Catholic, but ten percent were Jewish.

Newspapers pictured these newcomers as "greenhorns" who knew nothing. Sometimes they were portrayed as dangerous aliens. Other times these people were caricatured as unable or unwilling to adjust to life in America or to assimilate easily.

All of this was soon proved to be not true. Only one third were actually illiterate, and 90 percent of those who could not speak English learned to do so in less than ten years after they arrived. Their stamina helped make America an industrial giant and the world's leading economic power.

The Marriage Search

So many men arrived during the new immigration that marriageable women became needed by new ethnic communities. Many men saved their money to pay for the passage of women they intended to marry.

But this did not always work. Women who promised to join men sometimes married someone else. Immigrant men alone in the United States often met immigrant women. But thousands of immigrant men (often on the basis of a photograph) paid for the passage to America of their brides-to-be.

This immigrant bride arrived on the Baltic *in 1907.*

Religious and ethnic leaders in the United States warned that only marriages within one's own ethnic or religious community insured community stability and cultural survival. But the sons of immigrants, and then the daughters, sometimes chose to date and marry people of other nationalities, religions, and races. These intermarriages were seen as a threat by each ethnic group, particularly close-knit communities of Jews, Italians, Lebanese, Syrians, and Armenians. Intermarriage was a flash point in the "Americanization" process. And it was part of a larger quarrel immigrants had with a relentless American culture and its new values. ■

To Return Home?

Some immigrants planned to return home with enough cash to be a success in the Old World. And many did return home, particularly single young men. In the 1880s about 30 percent returned; in the 1890s, 35 percent; and by 1910, 38 percent. Irish or Jewish immigrants were most likely to stay, Romanians and Hungarians most likely to return.

Returning by Europeans was often related to U.S. business cycles. During periods of high U.S. unemployment, the jobless packed up and left for their ancestral homes. Many came back when jobs increased again. ■

These settlers arrived when America did not offer limitless opportunities. Good jobs and chances for advancement were few. Factory work was dull and routine. Periodic business depressions caused sudden, large-scale unemployment.

The newcomers entered the urban labor market when competition for high-paying positions was sharp. For the most part, they lacked the education and skills for economic advancement. They had few relatives or friends in high political or business positions, few who could help them rise quickly. Only a few ethnic groups such as the Armenians, Jews, Lebanese, and Syrians arrived with some experience of urban life and commercial enterprises.

The new immigrants came at a turning point in American growth. Bosses rarely knew their workers. Class animosity often divided management and labor. "I can hire one half the working class to kill the other half," boasted the millionaire industrialist Jay Gould.

Corporations showed little interest in their workers. Instead, these businesses sought to maximize profits.

To lower wages, plant managers often tried to pit one racial, religious, or ethnic minority against another to keep the pot of hostility boiling. A labor paper reported that employers were "keeping up a constant war of the races." Bosses placed spies among their employees so they could report on "troublemakers" — any who urged workers to organize unions.

CHAPTER 2

THE GREAT MIGRATIONS TO URBAN AMERICA

In urban America the newcomers often lived in slums called ghettoes. No laws told one where to live in America, but each ethnic group tended to stay together. Families from a European village often settled in a particular neighborhood or street.

These neighborhoods welcomed other people, and their ghetto populations rarely had more than half of the dominant minority. In New York City, Italian American vegetable peddlers served Jewish neighborhoods, Jewish American tailors served Italian neighborhoods, and Irish Americans sold wares in Syrian American neighborhoods in Boston. Greek and Chinese restaurants were accepted and popular in many different ethnic neighborhoods.

Three quarters of arriving immigrants settled in cities, where by 1910, they constituted one seventh of the U.S. population. This meant that 45 million people — almost half the total U.S. population — lived in cities, and 20 million were foreign-born.

Since many immigrants lived among relatives and friends, apartments were crowded. But they were still expensive. In 1910 in Chicago an apartment of seven rooms cost whites $25. For African Americans, seven similar rooms cost $37.50.

Immigrants were drawn to politics for reasons that went beyond a love of democracy. Since they were poor and desperate for work and a place to live, many easily fell into the hands of city political bosses. Many city political machines were run by Irish Americans, some of whom had arrived only a generation or two earlier. In return for the votes of newcomers, these politicians saw that the immigrants had jobs and that families found apartments. They provided legal help to immigrants who faced jail.

An early print shows Jewish American immigrants taking part in a political campaign.

The newcomers felt at ease with the local politicians and their practical city political machines. After all, these were Americans who were helping the immigrants solve life's basic needs. Few immigrants were won over by reformers who talked about democracy but disliked foreigners.

Other groups of people besides European immigrants were reshaping America's urban landscape at the turn of the century. Canadians were moving southward and Mexicans and South Americans northward into the United States.

From 1900 to 1930, 700,000 Mexicans were driven to the United States by poverty and by the turmoil and violence of the Mexican Revolution that began in 1910. Others were attracted by jobs paying far more than labor in Mexico.

Many Mexican Americans left their homes in the southwestern states for work in cities. Some sought jobs in Detroit auto plants, Chicago and Gary steel and meat plants, and Pennsylvania and Ohio steel mills. By the 1920s, Chicago's Mexican American population had soared from 4, 000 to 20,000.

By 1930, so many Mexican American men had taken industrial jobs that one in every four worked in a factory. Most wives and teenage daughters had to work, and of these about 45 percent had jobs in domestic and personal service. Others worked in food and other packaging plants. Only five percent held sales positions. Mexican American women earned less than men and less than white women.

Mexican Americans found little upward mobility. Bosses and foremen denied them advancement over whites. Still a Mexican

Pancho Villa, a Mexican revolutionary figure.

Old Immigration and New Countries

People still emigrated from such western European countries as Ireland, Germany, and France, and many of these immigrants also settled in cities. After 1890, hundreds of young women arrived from Finland. Usually traveling alone, they took jobs as housekeepers in such large cities as New York, San Francisco, Boston, Los Angeles, and Chicago, and usually married Finnish American men.

Between 1870 and 1900, about 15,000 of Iceland's 75,000 people left for the United States. Most did not know English. They came with little money and soon took unskilled jobs either in factories or on the docks. ■

American middle class did emerge from work in the service industry. Others who ran small stores and restaurants or became schoolteachers also joined the middle class.

By the early 1920s, more than half the Chicanos and Mexican-born immigrants in the Southwest lived in urban centers. In 1930 they made up half the population of El Paso, almost half of San Antonio, and a fifth of Los Angeles. Their ghettoes were called barrios.

By the early 20th century, stability in some barrios had produced strong self-help societies. Some proudly traced their origins to long before the Mexican War of 1848. *La Alianza Hispano-Americana*, formed in 1894 in Tucson, Arizona, was the largest of the groups. In the early 20th century it claimed 20,000 members in many states.

Some groups battled segregation and discrimination in the United States. *La Orden de Hijos de America*, begun in 1920 in San Antonio, was made up of Chicano white-collar workers determined to win full American citizenship rights.

Another stream of immigrants crossed into the United States from Canada. Beginning in 1865, French Canadian societies were forming in America and holding conventions.

French Canadians were determined not to lose their language and identity. By 1891, in New England they had established many French-language parochial schools with thousands of pupils. By 1909, French-language schools in the United States had grown to 179 elementary and 28 high schools. The children who went to these schools spoke English better than their parents, had many friends who were not French Canadians, and were far more interested in American culture than their older relatives.

By 1900, 275,000 French Canadians labored in New England mills. By 1908, those living in Rhode Island had elected one of their own, Aram Pothier, to the governor's mansion.

Between 1911 and 1930, more than a million and a half Canadians, many of French heritage, had moved to the United States. Some made unusual contributions. Alfred Fuller arrived from Nova Scotia in 1903 with little money and an idea. In his sister's basement, he put together his own special brushes and sold them door-to-door for 25 cents each. The huge Fuller Brush Company was born.

Between 1910 and 1920, a vast African American migration left the rural South for urban centers throughout the country. An estimated half a million people left the rural South for jobs in the North. This exodus began around 1915 as boll weevils wormed their way through and destroyed southern crops. The next year the floods hit the southern states.

The black migration first began as a step from the rural to the urban South, to Atlanta, Birmingham, and Memphis. In Charleston, Savannah, Baton Rouge, Jacksonville, Montgomery, Vicksburg, and Shreveport, African Americans became a majority. Men became urban laborers, and women took jobs as domestics, nursemaids, and cooks. There was little chance for advancement.

Urban life offered African Americans more opportunities than their rural kinfolk had, and some climbed into the middle class. In 1900 Booker T. Washington organized the National Negro Business League. By 1907, it had recruited hundreds of small entrepreneurs in its 320 thriving branches across the country.

African Americans in the South combined resources to finance business cooperatives in Atlanta, Hampton, Jacksonville, and Chattanooga. By 1914, 45 black banks, often affiliated with fraternal societies, had opened. Since they catered to a population without savings, or capital, or good jobs, most of these African American banks had short lives.

As the world war in Europe (1914-1918) dried up the stream of immigrants that industries had counted on for labor, black people began to head northward for jobs. The North offered powerful attractions for families who lived in the rural South without hope. "I want to come North where I can educate my three little children also my wife," wrote a black Mississippi lumber worker to a Chicago newspaper.

Most Blacks were pleased with city jobs. "Mrs. L." had been a maid in the South, but said, "they almost make you a slave." In Chicago she found a good job in a mail-order house. At age 14, "Miss T." had cooked for whites in Georgia. At 22 she had a job in a Chicago box factory. She made good wages in her new life but found that she couldn't save anything because "there are so many places to go."

After two years at a Kentucky high school and holding a janitor's job, "C.W." left for Chicago and a job in a foundry:

I'm an expert now and make as much as any man in the place. I can quit any time I want to, but the longer I work the more money it is for me, so I usually work eight or nine hours a day. I am planning to educate my girl with the best of them, buy a home before I'm too old, and make life comfortable for my family. There is more chance here to learn a trade than in the South. I live better, can save more, and feel more like a man.

During this era of the great migrations, the federal government continued its policy of confining Native Americans on reservations. By the 20th century, violent Indian resistance had ended. The government was pursuing a policy called "assimilation," or a full-scale effort to dominate or eliminate Native American cultures.

Federal officials sought to end Indian common ownership of land. In an age of industrialism, they insisted that Native Americans become farmers or ranchers. Indians lost much of their land and became wageworkers instead.

Federal authorities used education to root out Native American culture by sending Indian children to boarding schools far from

The government Indian school at Swinomish Reservation in the state of Washington.

their parents. In 1908 Richard Pratt, founder and director of the Carlisle School, revealed how he undermined each child's Indian heritage in Carlisle's schoolrooms and dormitories.

> The rooms held three to four each, and it was arranged that no two of the same tribe were placed in the same room. This not only helped in the acquirement of English but broke up tribal and race clannishness, a most important victory in getting the Indian toward real citizenship.

Yvonne Leaf, a Dakota, remembered being "all mixed up. Why can't I be an Indian. I wanted to live with my parents." Sioux Bulah Robeson found Carlisle preferable to reservation life where

> We went hungry. We had no shoes to wear. At school we got three meals a day. We were given shoes.

In 1991 Ted Montoya still spoke angrily about white education.

> We were sent into a scary new world to be taught how to be a better American. Our culture was bleached out and we were made into European-style farmers. We marched to work, marched to classes. We got a whipping for a lot of things. Kids ran away every day. Nearby farmers were paid $5 for every one they caught and returned.... I vowed never to send my children to Indian boarding schools.

White educators often complained about Native Americans "going back to the blanket," or returning to former ways despite efforts to convert them to capitalist, republican, and Christian goals.

Many Native American societies had adapted Christianity to their ancient practices or developed new religious forms. They struggled to preserve ancient languages. Of hundreds of these languages only a dozen died out, and many Indians through a vigorous effort were able to adhere to their ceremonial life.

By 1928, a U.S. government report, *The Problem Of Indian Administration*, called the assimilationist policy a failure. It agreed that reservation life was characterized by poverty, poor health, and lack of education.

NEW YORK CITY'S LOWER EAST SIDE

By the 1880s, New York City's Lower East Side stretched from the East River to Broadway and from Chambers Street uptown to 14th Street. It became home for thousands of newly arrived immigrants, first Jews, and then Italians and Chinese.

In the 1830s the Lower East Side was an Irish American community and in the 1840s a community of free African Americans. German Americans arrived after 1848 and created an exciting climate of "free education" and culture. Newcomers found the area's crowded streets congenial and appreciated the fact that rent for its five-story walk-up apartments was cheap.

By 1865, the Lower East Side had 15,000 tenements, and 480,000 people crowded into them. Some 3,000 people lived in one block.

A Christmas at Gotham Court, photographed by Jacob Riis.

Gotham Court, 36 Cherry Street, offered families apartments of two rooms, one 9 by 14 feet and the other 9 by 6 feet. There was no plumbing or heat. An average of eight people shared an apartment. In 1900 Gotham Court was still considered a comfortable home for a large family.

Not far away, on Elizabeth and Mott streets, bigger families found three rooms — 4 by 11 feet, 8 by 7 feet, and 8 by 7 feet. Few of these rooms had windows, and the hallways had water puddles and were often filled with filth and stench. In the face of these conditions, both adults and children found their escape in

a lively street life in good weather. To help pay the rent, many families took in boarders who slept on fire escapes, or on rows of mattresses on the floor or on the roof.

Among residents of the Lower East Side bad news was common. Unemployment, early death, industrial accidents, tuberculosis, and typhoid fever were everyday occurrences. Many babies did not live to reach their first birthday, but the Lower East Side also offered many factory jobs, and by the year 1900, parts of the Lower East Side were more densely populated than Bombay, India.

A 1910 school for immigrants of all ages.

The new immigrants who arrived sought to expand the educational efforts of earlier German American residents. New ethnic groups added new subjects of study. For a few pennies, and sometimes for nothing, one could take courses in anything from women's suffrage to vegetarianism to political philosophies. Radical views and sects were fully represented.

Protest speeches and songs increasingly were heard in many languages and accents. There was agitation for the 8-hour workday in the 1880s and marches to show support for striking workers in nearby Brooklyn or distant Idaho at the turn of the century.

The dominant language of the Jewish residents of the Lower East Side was Yiddish (a German dialect spoken by Jews), and its most familiar voice was Abraham Cahan, a Jewish Lithuanian radical who fled Russia to escape arrest. He spoke at meetings of the Propaganda Association for the Dissemination of Socialist Ideas Among Immigrant Jews. In 1897 he began the Jewish *Daily Forward*. It gave Yiddish-speaking newcomers sage advice and promoted the values of attending school, learning English, and absorbing American ways. Until his death in 1951, Cahan edited the *Forward* and offered his advice on many subjects.

Some Lower East Side residents paid little attention to the political turmoil around them. They had more immediate goals. Marcus Loew was born in 1870 to a poverty-stricken Austrian American waiter and a German American widow with two children from a previous marriage. He later recalled these early days.

I was poor, but so was everyone around me.... It's an advantage to be poor in one sense. That's why so many successes come from the East Side. The ones with talent for better things have every incentive there to exercise them.

By the time he was 35, young Loew had made his fortune turning storefronts into new movie theaters. He was among a number of residents of the Lower East Side who hit pay dirt and then moved uptown.

Hester Street was a hub of activity on New York City's Lower East Side.

21

CHAPTER 4

THE BALTIC PEOPLES

The Baltic States were ruled by the Russian czar in the latter part of the 19th century. The people of the Baltic states — Latvia, Lithuania, and Estonia — lived unhappily under the control of Russia.

By 1884, 15,000 Lithuanians had left for America. Most were young men, some unmarried and some married, who planned to work and then return home to their families. Many settled in Pennsylvania coal mining towns, but some chose to live on New England farms, and others settled in large cities like Boston, New York, and Baltimore.

Within two decades, relatives in America encouraged an even larger exodus from Lithuania. New arrivals spread out to take work in New Jersey oil refineries, Chicago garment shops, the Maine and Michigan forest industries, and steel mills in Pittsburgh, Detroit, and Cleveland.

Following a revolt in the early 1900s against Russian domination, 5,000 Latvians fled their homeland, and most came to America. The Latvian population in this country suddenly doubled.

Some Latvian immigrants were actors, such as Mice Niedze, who arrived in 1906 after a stage career in Riga, Latvia's capital. He became a star among his fellow exiles in New York. In a 30-year period he played some 400 roles on the stage.

Milda Salnais was sentenced by Russian authorities at age 19 to a Siberian prison for life, but she fled Latvia for Switzerland and then immigrated to America. She gave inspiring lectures on freedom in America's Latvian communities. She later embarked on a career in journalism and in 1917 returned to Latvia as an Associated Press correspondent .

By 1908, 2,000 Latvian Americans in Lincoln County, Wisconsin, had created a farm community, where they cleared the land of trees and planted crops. Farms ranged in size from a few dozen acres to more than a hundred acres each. Disputes arose

The Intellectual Who Shaped a Culture

Jonas Sliupas, born in 1861, became an intellectual leader for Lithuanians throughout Europe while still in his twenties. In East Prussia he edited *The Dawn*, the first Lithuanian nationalist periodical. To escape arrest by German and Russian police, he fled his homeland for Brooklyn, New York, in 1884.

Within a year of his arrival, Sliupas was publishing *The Lithuanian Voice*, one of his people's earliest American periodicals. Through this journal and with his visits to Atlantic coast communities, he urged fellow Lithuanians to stop following the lead of Polish Americans and to create their own institutions.

From New York to Baltimore, Sliupas organized various Lithuanian American educational and self-help societies. In 1886 he started the Alliance of All Lithuanians in America, his people's first federation of associations. In 1889 he formed the Lithuanian Scientific Society, which also published a journal.

Sliupas's paper and Alliance both failed. Then, the man who had first cooperated with Lithuanian Catholic clerics launched a campaign against their "domination." His newly formed Lithuanian Educational Society and his *New Age* journal demanded "free thought" by which he meant the rejection of established religions.

The Lithuanian Educational Society faded and so did the *New Age*, but Sliupas was far from discouraged. In 1900 he formed the Lithuanian Alliance of Free-thinkers, which lasted 15 years.

In 1905 he became a founder of the Lithuanian Socialist Party. During and after World War I, he spoke out for national self-determination. In 1919 he helped write a famous Captive Nations Declaration for Lithuanians and all Baltic peoples under foreign rule.

Before Sliupas took the lead there was little Lithuanian spirit or nationalism. He was the proud, daring father of these secular movements. His efforts cemented their foundations and sparked a great outpouring of nationalist, socialist, and independent societies and papers. He died in 1944, as his homeland was liberated from Nazi Germany only to fall under the domination of the Soviet Union. ■

when recent, younger immigrants with new ideas clashed with earlier arrivals. The colony began to collapse, and people left for urban centers.

In 1913 Anna Enke at the University of Chicago became the first Latvian American woman to graduate from an American college. She then took a job as a professor of Romance Languages.

The number of Estonians who reached America is hard to determine. The U.S. Congress estimated that, by 1890, more than

5,000 people were of Estonian descent, and by 1920, that figure rose to 69,200.

The earliest Estonian American organization was a Lutheran congregation started in South Dakota in 1897. A church in rural Wisconsin followed and then a school in Montana. Other arrivals settled down in Colorado, Wyoming, Washington, and Oregon.

A pioneer Estonian missionary, Lutheran Reverend Hans Rebane, arrived in 1896 to found congregations in Philadelphia, Boston, New York, South Dakota, and Wisconsin. Rebane also published a newspaper from 1897 until his death in 1911.

Many Estonian immigrants preferred secular to religious groups, and in 1898 they formed the Estonian American Beneficial Society in New York City. It sponsored cultural and social activities. In the early 1900s other self-help groups were formed in Portland, Oregon, San Francisco, and Philadelphia. A revolution in Russia in 1905 failed, and many Estonians fled to the United States. The new arrivals infused the Estonian American community with a prolabor orientation that lasted for years.

CHAPTER 5

FROM THE BALKANS AND GREECE

The Balkan countries, which stretch from central Europe to the Mediterranean and Adriatic seas, were often dominated by foreign powers who mistreated local populations in the years before World War I. Millions of immigrants fled to the United States from Europe's huge Austro-Hungarian and Ottoman (Turkish) Balkan empires and from Greece. Some families left starvation and unemployment behind, while others fled ethnic oppression to seek justice and opportunity in the United States.

Although the first Albanian to settle in the United States, Kole Kristofor, arrived in the 1880s, it was not until the early 20th century that a large number of Albanians arrived. The first group of Albanians were mostly single men with a sprinkling of married men. These Albanians were Christian Tosks from the southern part of Albania.

An Italian woman of Albanian Greek ancestry.

Most Albanian immigrants planned to return to their families in Albania with their American earnings. They worked hard in New England textile mills, shoe factories, and shipyards, and Boston was their port of entry and their major urban center.

From Massachusetts and New York, men seeking industrial jobs spread out to Cleveland, Pittsburgh, Detroit, and Chicago. In time most Albanian immigrants decided to remain in America, become citizens, and settle in cities rather than in rural areas.

As wives arrived from Europe, Albanian American communities stabilized. Old ways were preserved by families and celebrated in holiday picnics. These offered traditional vegetable pies, and songs and dances in bright native costumes.

Albanian Americans soon began to form self-help societies and to send money to their homeland. At first, ancient Albanian rituals were preserved by families and the Albanian church. But soon children educated in American schools began to climb American ladders of success. Some were able to step into the middle class by opening groceries, restaurants, and cleaning establishments.

Churches offered immigrants language classes that taught many Albanian Americans to read and write their own language for the first time. In 1906 the first U.S. Albanian paper, *Kombi*, was published in Boston, and others soon followed.

Many Albanians returned to their fatherland following World War I. But in 1920 some 6,000 Americans said Albanian was their mother tongue.

Between 1900 and 1910, an estimated 50,000 Bulgarians, mostly single, rural men, arrived in the United States. Most had little education and few urban skills. They intended to earn the cash to return home and buy land or begin a small business.

Early Bulgarian migration is hard to measure for a number of reasons. U.S. officials listed them under other countries such as Turkey or Romania. Moreover, some entered the United States through Mexico or Canada or carried passports from Russia, Greece, Turkey, and Romania.

Many Bulgarians settled in Granite City, Illinois, and some worked in Pennsylvania steel mills, on western railroads, and in factories in the northeastern states. Once in the United States, Bulgarian Americans often began a *boort*, a boardinghouse run by immigrant couples. In a *boort*, about a dozen or so immigrants rented two rooms, one for sleeping and the other for cooking and living. They also began *kafnes*, or coffeehouses.

These Romanian shepherds were among many rural Europeans who arrived at the turn of the century.

By 1907, Granite City had its first Bulgarian-language paper, the *National Herald*, which printed a daily edition between 1913 and 1926. In 1909 the city's Bulgarian Americans started their first Orthodox church. Bulgarian American societies were formed on the basis of certain regions in the fatherland. But by the 1910s, these societies began to merge into Bulgarian national societies. Then, in 1913, the first female group, Bulgarian Women in America, was formed in the United States.

Slav sisters (far left photo) and Slav woman and husband arriving at Ellis Island.

Beginning in 1900, tens of thousands of Greek citizens sailed to America from their homes in Turkey and Greece. Those who left Turkey were usually educated people from cities, and some were successful businessmen. Many from Greece were single, unskilled men from rural Peloponnesian villages driven away by crop failures.

Between 1911 and 1920, a vast migration pushed one fourth of Greece's laborers to the United States. These early arrivals sent back money that paid the passage to America for their families and for many others.

Rural Greeks settled in urban America. Rather than take farming jobs, they preferred to turn city neighborhoods into warm, gregarious places reminiscent of their homeland. Many settled in the northeastern states where they worked in textile and steel mills, tanneries, on railroads, or in coal mines. Some came to Florida where they fished for a living. In California, some started small businesses — restaurants, fruit and vegetable stands, flower shops, and candy stores.

The first known Greek restaurant opened in New York City before the Civil War, and by the early 20th century, Greek restaurants had become a traditional family business and a first step up the economic ladder for small entrepreneurs.

Greek American parents were offended when their children showed little interest in Greece. To counter this lack of interest, they

Chicago's Greek American Women

...Greek women adapt themselves very quickly to American customs. A Greek Women's Club has been meeting at Hull House once a week and a Greek Women's Philanthropic Society has been formed there by the more prosperous, who expect to help in various ways the unfortunate members of their colony. This charitable organization is eagerly encouraged by the men, for the Greeks, although extremely shrewd in their business dealings, are at the same time generous. They give liberally to one another in times of sickness or unemployment.... When three small Greek children were left without homes, it was not difficult to find Greek families in the neighborhood of Hull House who were willing to receive and care for them temporarily or indefinitely.

Unlike the Italian women, they do not work outside their own homes or at a sweatshop. Out of the 246 Greek women and girls over 15 who were visited in this investigation, only five were found to be at work. This is not alone because the Greek man usually succeeds in business, but because he considers it a disgrace for his wife or his sister to work.... The women are good housekeepers. The Greek houses are almost uniformly clean and comfortable, and the women and children neatly dressed.

Hull House survey in 1909 on "Greek women in Chicago." ◼

instituted Greek language and cultural schools. With priests as instructors, classes began in church basements. Greece's Independence Day, March 25, 1821, was soon celebrated in many Greek American neighborhoods.

Many old-world customs were planted in the new soil. In both middle-class and workers' homes, fathers and brothers insisted that women remain at home and do the housework rather than take outside jobs. Men tried to protect this "sacred tradition."

Life for Greek Americans was not an uninterrupted upward climb. In 1909 a mob drove 1,200 Greek immigrants out of Omaha, Nebraska, destroying their homes and businesses. They had triggered local fears of job competition.

Greek Americans found time to respond to the needs of Greece itself. The Panhellenic Union helped 42,000 volunteers return during the Balkan Wars in 1912 and 1913 to serve Greece as soldiers. Most returned to the United States, many with new wives. But about 48 percent of Greeks who returned to the homeland remained.

CHAPTER 6

ARMENIANS: FROM GENOCIDE TO HOPE

Armenians are Christians whose homelands were in northern Turkey and southern Russia. In Turkey they faced armed assaults encouraged by the government, and survivors of these attacks were often forced to convert to Islam. In 1909 attacks on Armenians led to 30,000 deaths and only halted when the United States and other major world powers vigorously protested.

In 1915 the assaults escalated into outright genocide, a systematic effort to annihilate an entire people. By 1916, 1,800,000 Armenians had died, and a million more had fled to safety.

One of those who strongly protested this genocide was the U.S. ambassador to Turkey, Henry Morgenthau, a Jewish American. Morganthau organized "Near East Relief" to aid Armenian victims and publicized the plight of Armenian families under Turkey's rule.

In 1913 more than 9,000 Armenian refugees left for the United States. Most were single men between 14 and 45. They were aided by the Armenian Students Association, which was formed after the 1909 massacres to offer loans and scholarships.

Those who left in the first decades of the century were united by their language, by the Armenian Apostolic church, and by a love for the homelands they had to leave behind. Between 1900 and 1914, 50,000 Armenians came to America. Armenian newcomers often arrived with some trade or skill. More than one in every three had training as a tailor, a shoemaker, or a carpenter. About 40 percent of the Armenian immigrants had lived in towns in Turkey and Russia, and the vast majority were able to read and write. Unlike ethnic groups who intended to return home, Armenian refugees knew they had lost any chance to return to their homelands. They came to stay.

Armenian Americans brought a dedication to higher education

and made striking use of American schools. In 1921 the percentage of Armenians in colleges exceeded that of any other immigrant group. Many Armenian Americans graduated to find white-collar and professional jobs.

The Armenian experience in America was not an uninterrupted success. In 1909 the federal government tried to prevent Armenians from gaining U.S. citizenship by claiming they were "Asiatics." But a federal judge classified them as Caucasians eligible for citizenship. In Fresno, California, Armenian immigrants encountered anger from neighboring communities that resented the success of the newcomers.

Armenian Americans, like other immigrant groups, faced severe problems of identity. Men outnumbered women, and community efforts sought to promote marriages to Armenian women. Children were urged to retain their language. But in school they learned a new language which they needed for success in business. In schools and parks, they were introduced to clothes, foods, and sports that pulled them away from parental domination. Few cared

---

Armenian American Accomplishments

In 1920 in *Outlook* magazine, Reverend Joseph Kafafian Thompson, a graduate of Yale Divinity School, proudly summarized Armenian American accomplishments.

The Armenian farmers have made good in California. Armenians handle 80 percent of the oriental rugs that come to America. There are over one hundred Armenian clergymen; 39 of these preach to American congregations. The number of Armenian doctors and dentists exceeds 200. Armenian lawyers now in active practice number 15. There are a great number of engineers, chemists, architects, and editors of Armenian and American papers....

The number of Armenian students in American colleges and universities in 1916 was 234. When we consider the fact that there are less than 100,000 Armenians in America, this is a better record than that of any other foreign people and is as good as that of the native-born American.

By the time this article appeared, Armenia faced a new problem. It was in the hands of the Soviet Union. A new wave of immigrants was on its way to America. ■

to learn Armenian, to attend church, or to meet the usual demands set by their parents.

Armenian Americans formed fraternal groups to preserve their identity and culture. Some societies offered reading rooms, ran conventions, and raised funds for churches, schools, and hospitals in the regions they had left behind.

The Armenian General Benevolent Union began in 1908 and in five years had a membership of 8,500. It sought to help Armenian refugees throughout the world. In 1910 the Armenian Red Cross, which was devoted to education and relief, was formed by Armenian American women. It denied membership to males.

Religious institutions also grew with new arrivals. By 1916, the Armenian American community supported 10 churches and 17 priests. Women played a prominent role in church matters. But church attendance had begun to lapse, and few Armenian Americans observed the traditional 160 fast days in their new homeland. To regain leadership among the young, church figures began to organize clubs for men, for the young, and for women.

CHAPTER 7

THE JEWISH MIGRATION

An immigrant Russian Jew, photographed standing before what he hoped would be his "golden door."

From 1882 to World War I, 2 million European Jews came to America. Many were driven by starvation in the Austro-Hungarian Empire. Almost 75 percent of the Jewish immigrants had to flee pogroms, or mob attacks, organized by Russian officials in eastern Russia and in what is now Poland. In 1891 Moscow drove out 20,000 Jews, then St. Petersburg and Kharkov drove out their Jews. In 1903 and 1905, as pogroms increased, thousands more fled.

Perhaps more than any other European ethnic group, Jews landed to find a network of societies prepared to ease their adjustment. The Hebrew Immigrant Aid Society (HIAS) formed in 1892 and took on the task of receiving and assisting Jewish arrivals. Young Jewish women who were alone in cities could turn to the National Council of Jewish Women for advice and for a place to stay.

The massive Jewish migrations from eastern and southern Europe soon attracted the attention of earlier, established German Jews in America. Some had found success in business, real estate, and finance. At first some of the wealthy kept their distance and referred to the newcomers disparagingly as "Orientals," or angrily as "Kikes."

However, some of the prior arrivals also wanted to ease the Americanization of their fellow Jews by helping them adjust to the new land. These German Americans sought ways to obliterate the newcomers' old-world habits and their reliance on Yiddish.

In New York City the device chosen for Americanization was the Educational Alliance, a settlement house on the Lower East Side sponsored by wealthy German Americans. The Alliance prepared Jewish children for public schools by first banning Yiddish and teaching basic English. For adults it offered night classes in English, cooking, sewing, Greek and Roman history, and American Civics.

Jewish immigrant children.

The Alliance's staff presented astounding opportunities. For families crammed into small, dingy New York City apartments, it offered space.

"The Alliance gave me a new life — I had never seen such big rooms before," said Zero Mostel. He learned to paint in its art classes and later became a famous movie actor.

But the staff at the Alliance also force-fed American patriotism to each Jew who joined. Eugene Lyons, who later became a famous writer, recalled:

> We were Americanized about as gently as horses are broken in. In the whole crude process, we sensed a disrespect for the alien traditions in our homes and came unconsciously to resent and despise those traditions, good and bad alike, because they seemed insuperable barriers between ourselves and our adopted land.

In time the Educational Alliance began to change. Being close to the Yiddish heritage, its sponsors realized, did not hinder good citizenship or undermine one's love of America. The Alliance staff allowed Yiddish in its classes, and it even translated the Declaration of Independence into Yiddish. The Alliance accepted the cultural diversity of Europe's Jews and no longer saw their adherence to ancient traditions as a threat.

To surmount hurdles they found in America, Jewish immigrants and their American children created their own ladders to success. Jewish workers entered the clothing industry, and a few invested their savings in early factories. Soon Jewish American entrepreneurs dominated the leading clothing firms. Cash from this field flowed into a host of other businesses.

Some European Jews eagerly entered the field of entertainment. Rabbi Baline's family sailed in 1893 from Russia after an anti-Semitic mob had burned down their home. Baline had saved his seven girls and boys from the fire. As Israel, age four, sat on a blanket and watched the flames consume his home, it became a sight he never forgot.

The Baline family sailed to America and settled on New York's Lower East Side. Israel worked as a newsboy and a singing waiter and began to write songs. In 1911, as Irving Berlin, he wrote "Alexander's Ragtime Band." He composed hundreds of popular songs, including "God Bless America" and "White Christmas."

Some immigrants, following in the footsteps of "Mother" Marm Mandelbaum in New York City, took the fast lane to riches as criminals. A fence for stolen goods in the 1870s, Mandelbaum had solid links to police officers. Teaching techniques of burglary, safe-blowing, and blackmail became her specialty.

Children's class at the Portland, Oregon, Temple Beth Israel in 1898.

Monk Eastman (born Edward Osterman) and his Jewish band, Nathan Kaplan, Spanish Johnny, and Little Kishky, became the Williamsburg gang. They allied with the Irish American leaders of Tammany Hall. To poor families trying to make a living, these criminals were a *shonda*, a disgrace that poisoned their communities .

Most Jews settled in New York City where in 1920 they totaled 26 percent of the population. Arriving poor, they had to adjust to crowded slums and slept four to a room. Rates for tuberculosis, nervous disorders, and suicides were high among American Jews, but the group had a much lower death rate than other newcomers.

An important self-help organization, the Anti-Defamation League (ADL), was organized in 1914 to combat anti-Semitic propaganda and employment discrimination in the United States. The ADL issued books and educational materials to inform citizens about Jewish contributions to American life.

By then, "Jewish quotas" had been set by colleges, businesses, and social clubs to limit exactly how many Jews were to be admitted. Harvard University's president announced that a quota was necessary to keep down the number of Jewish Americans who entered.

But Jews, like Irish and Italian Americans, found they encountered little discrimination in the boxing and entertainment fields. Talented Jewish, Irish, and Italian American performers lit up American vaudeville stages at the turn of the century and went on to popularity in the early days of the motion picture industry.

Movies were highly popular in Jewish neighborhoods. The first screening of a film took place in 1896 at Koster and Bial's New York City Music Hall.

In 1905 nickelodeon movies (which cost only a nickel) were developed, and by the end of the decade, one in five Americans attended movies once a week. In New York 42 of the 123 playhouses were located on the Jewish East Side. Films were sandwiched between Jewish and Irish American comedians, singers, dancers, jugglers, and magicians. The films were five minutes long, had predictable plots, and were made up of visual tricks.

Jewish Americans also made early contributions to American medicine. In 1887 Willy Myer invented the cystoscope, an instrument that conducted tests by probing the body's internal organs. In 1888 Bernard Sachs discovered and then tried to find a cure for a fatal brain disease that afflicted Jewish children. He was the first physician to write about nervous disorders of the young. The next year Simon Baruch conducted the first successful removal of a human appendix.

Jewish immigrants at prayer.

CHAPTER 8

CZECH, SLOVAK, AND POLISH AMERICANS

Czech immigrants were evenly divided between choosing city or rural life. Half of the immigrants settled in cities, and the other half struck out for farms in Nebraska, Wisconsin, Iowa, Minnesota, and Texas.

In the last quarter of the 19th century, Slovaks began to arrive here in great numbers, and by 1886, they were publishing many papers and magazines. By 1889, they had formed 40 lodges along religious lines: Roman Catholic, Greek Orthodox, Lutheran, and Calvinist. In 1890 a National Slovak Society was founded. Then Slovak women, excluded from these lodges, formed their own organization.

These Slovak girls were photographed at Ellis Island.

Early Slovak American immigrants usually became factory or mine workers who labored 10 or 12 hours for $1.50 a day. Family members turned their homes into boardinghouses so they could take in arriving relatives. Then newly arrived strangers also became renters. Everyone enjoyed home cooking at the family table, and each guest was treated as part of the family.

Slovak American immigrants also made strong efforts to retain their ancient customs. Baptisms were elaborate, and weddings lasted from two days to two weeks. In a sort of fund-raising marathon, a bride would dance with each guest who then offered the new couple a monetary gift. During their first years of marriage, newlyweds lived with parents and then tried to find a new home next door or nearby.

In 1890 Polish workers in Europe labored from sunrise to sundown for 12 cents a day. Their relatives and friends in the U.S. made 90 cents a day as farm laborers and even more as either unskilled miners or factory workers. A Polish exodus to America began.

Polish Americans and other immigrants did a lot of their trading on the street.

In Pennsylvania's anthracite mining district a Polish American also did something his European relatives could never do. He saved about $135 a year and sent most of this to his relations in Poland.

Polish Americans also dutifully wrote letters to their families across the sea, and these letters invariably described a wondrous land of abundance. The arrival of cash and letters had an enormous impact on emigration. By 1914, 2 million Poles had arrived in the United States. Most of them joined relatives already here.

By the 1890s, Chicago had 40,000 Polish Americans, the largest foreign-born community in the city, and was known as America's Warsaw. Polish families averaged six children. The newcomers created a host of self-help groups. In 1880 the Polish National Alliance was formed, and the next year the first Polish American cooperative store was begun by people pooling their resources. Soon other Polish immigrants formed loan associations to make land purchases. By 1900, Polish Americans had formed 14 major societies. Next, Polish American doctors, lawyers, and teachers started professional associations.

Chicago's Polish American women decided to strike out and form their own societies. In 1898 these many groups and committees were consolidated into the Polish Women's Alliance.

Pay was higher than in Poland, but so were expenses. So men encouraged women who did not have to supervise children to go to work. However, men also insisted that women's jobs be close to home. Older women became domestics in private homes or worked in hotels, laundries, or restaurants. Younger women took jobs as clerks in local candy stores. In some mining regions, women were able to find work in nearby textile factories. In Chicago women did labeling and other light work in meat-packing plants, near their men, but in cleaner surroundings. In 1900 pay for Polish American women and girls was about $3 a week or less.

Like many other immigrants, those from Poland first thought of themselves as sojourners, or visitors, who planned to return home. But gradually, some used the money they had saved to buy American homes and farms. Urban laborers managed the change to farm life in states such as Maryland, Pennsylvania, Nebraska, New Jersey, Minnesota, Wisconsin, Connecticut, and New York.

Immigrant Poles and Russians being vaccinated aboard ship in New York Harbor in 1881.

But most Polish Americans resided in cities. There they built churches named after their favorite saints. Some churches began in local stores or inns. The number of Polish parishes rose from 17 in 1870 to 390 in 1900.

Most immigrants from Poland were devoted to the Catholic church. However, some embraced a form of religious nationalism. The Polish Catholic church had to meet the challenge of a rising secularism and nationalism in Polish communities.

This secularism grew among working-class Polish Americans and took the form of devotion to labor unions, even when clergymen and community leaders might be against unionism. Polish Americans became an early source of the United Mine Workers of America, which was formed in 1890.

The first American Polish newspaper, *Echo from Poland*, appeared in 1863. By the turn of the century, it had been followed by half a dozen other papers. By printing poetry and the classics of Polish literature, newspapers helped keep the Polish language and culture alive from one American generation to the next.

The links between Poland and America were cemented by the millions of dollars Polish American workers sent back to Poland. Though this mainly was to the economic benefit of Poland, the country's officials sometimes resented the influx of dollars because it posed a threat to their power. This American cash also paid for more tickets to the United States.

CHAPTER 9

SWEATSHOPS AND SURVIVAL

By the first decade of the 20th century, "sweatshops," crowded factories where men, women, and children labored long hours, were a common part of the urban landscape. Sweatshop contractors also supplied machines to those forced to work at home. Usually these workers were women who had to care for infants, small children, and those who were ill or elderly.

Factories were squeezed into basements or upper floors of tenements. Neither a common language nor blood relations eased conditions. Girls could be fined 25 cents for giggling and 50 cents for staring out of windows or spending time in the bathroom. Many had to pay for thread or rent the tools required in their work.

Sweatshop machine operators worked 15 to 18 hours a day in a small room, often with a 6-year-old child assisting. Most often, sweatshop operators were paid for the pieces they completed so they would work fast. Employers sped up the work by reducing the price for each piece.

This sweatshop system had few safety precautions and no legal limitations. Writer Ernest Poole wrote of these night workers:

This immigrant Italian woman was photographed in 1910 by Lewis Hine.

Sweatshops such as this one were located in some ethnic ghetto neighborhoods.

Poor immigrant family members, including the children, had to work hard to help the family survive.

Some sing Yiddish songs — while they race. The women chat and laugh sometimes — while they race. For these are not yet dumb slaves, but intensely human beings — young, and straining every nerve of youth's vitality. Among operators twenty years is an active lifetime. Forty-five is old age. They make but half a living.

By 1900, approximately 150,000 Jewish Americans in New York City made their living in the garment industry. They produced half the nation's clothing. The average working woman in New York earned $6.50 a week, and men averaged $12. This left families with barely enough for rent and food.

Reformers tried to expose the most shameful conditions in sweatshops. In Chicago, state investigator Florence Kelley found people at work in crowded, foul, "ill-lighted, unventilated rooms." Her report described dampness, darkness, fumes, stench, filth, extreme cold or heat, poisonous gases, fire, danger, and death.

By 1909, Italian American women had joined Jews in the sweatshops. But Lower East Side women that year danced to a new, discontented beat. The International Ladies Garment Workers Union (ILGWU) was 8 years old, had a hundred members, and $4 in its treasury. But even young women who had not joined the ILGWU talked of a walkout, or leaving their jobs. It was brave talk.

In November 1909, a meeting at New York's Cooper Union brought out thousands of shirtwaist workers to discuss a strike. Samuel Gompers for the AFL and Mary Drier, an organizer for the Women's Trade Union League (WTUL), urged caution.

Then Clara Lemlich, a slim teenage striker, stood up to speak.

I am a working girl, one of these striking against intolerable conditions. I am tired of listening to speakers who talk in generalities. What we are here for is to decide whether or not to strike. I offer a resolution that a general strike be declared — now.

Clara Lemlich

Striking immigrant women in a proud, defiant march.

Lemlich's passionate speech in Yiddish electrified the audience, and thousands of hands in the air voted a strike. Jewish and Italian American women walked the picket lines. Aiding them were Mary Drier, social worker Lillian Wald, and the middle-class women of the WTUL. Rich women provided bail money for those women who were arrested — 723 in the first month.

The spirit on the picket line remained high even after men hired by employers attacked the pickets, knocked Lemlich and others to their knees, and pushed strikebreakers through their line. The women battled the strikebreakers as best they could.

At the women's union hall, milk and bread was given to those strikers with children. "There, for the first time in my comfortably sheltered, Upper West Side life," wrote a reporter, "I saw real hunger on the faces of my fellow Americans in the richest city in the world."

In ten weeks the strike was settled. There were improvements in conditions, but employers refused to recognize the ILGWU as the bargaining agent or representative of the strikers. But by now, the union had swelled from 100 to 10,000 members. Young Italian and Jewish American women had learned the power of unity.

Five months later, 60,000 male cloak makers called another strike. A poet, Morris Winchevsky, was the strike's chief fund-raiser. Leaflets were issued in Yiddish, English, and Italian. After six weeks, both sides agreed to settle the dispute peacefully.

Sweatshop misery did not end with a few successful strikes. The pain in sweatshop neighborhoods was part of the industrial system. People remained crowded in firetrap buildings. Tenements for the poor, and this included most immigrants, made up a third of New York City's housing. More than half the city's fires were in tenements.

In March 1911, a fire swept through the Triangle Shirtwaist Company near New York City's Washington Square. In the 18 minutes that the fire roared out of control on the ninth and tenth floors, it snuffed out the lives of 146 Jewish and Italian American immigrant women. Some died when they were unable to push open doors bolted to keep out union organizers. To escape the inferno, some leaped to their death. No net was strong enough to catch the plummeting bodies.

Immigrant Rose Schneiderman devoted her life to organizing women into unions and in the 1930s became a member of President Franklin Roosevelt's "brain trust."

One of those who rushed to the scene of the tragedy was 29-year-old Frances Perkins. The experience changed her life. She led the New York State Safety Commission and became an expert on factory hazards. In 1933 President Franklin D. Roosevelt appointed her Secretary of Labor, making her the first woman to serve in a presidential cabinet.

Rose Schneiderman, an immigrant and a union official, had tried to organize the Triangle women the year before the fire. Now she spoke at a memorial meeting for their dead:

The old inquisition had its rack and its thumbscrews and its instruments of torture with iron teeth. We know what these things are today: the iron teeth are our necessities, the thumbscrews are the high-powered and swift machinery close to which we must work, and the rack is here in the firetrap structures that will destroy us the minute they catch fire.

This is not the first time girls have been burned alive in this city. Every week I must learn of the untimely death of one of my sister workers. Every year thousands of us are maimed.

Public officials have only words of warning for us —

warning that we must be intensely orderly and must be intensely peaceable, and they have the workhouse just back of all their warnings. The strong hand of the law beats us back when we rise — back into conditions that make life unbearable.

Protest meetings over the Triangle tragedy drew huge audiences. Private individuals and charities donated money to surviving family members. New fire safety laws were passed in New York. But the sweatshops remained a part of ghetto life. And no one was found guilty or jailed for the Triangle Fire.

Children at Work

By 1910, more than 2 million immigrant children worked in poorly lighted and unsafe mines and mills. Children from age 6 and up labored 12 to 14 hours a day, 6 days a week, for 6 cents an hour.

Half of the children in New York City aged 5 to 18 could not attend school because they held jobs. Some labored in sweatshops. Others delivered messages, ran errands, shined shoes, or sold matches. In a Dunmore, Pennsylvania, silk mill, Helen Sissack, 11, worked from 6:30 P.M. to 6:30 A.M. for 3 cents an hour.

The accident rate for children in factories was double the adult rate. "Children are found in greater number," wrote Illinois factory inspector Florence Kelley, "where the conditions of labor are most dangerous to life and health." Her inspectors discovered children in tobacco factories suffering from nicotine poisoning.

In an Alabama textile mill, an official found a child "50 inches high and weighing perhaps 48 pounds, who works from 6 at night until 6 in the morning and is so tiny that she has to climb up on the spinning frame to reach the top row of spindles." Through the efforts of Kelley and other reformers, laws were finally passed in various states to prohibit child labor. ■

Children at work were children at risk and children denied an education.

C H A P T E R   1 0

FROM ITALIAN SHORES

More than 3 million Italians arrived at Ellis Island in the first two decades of the 20th century, and most of them were landless peasants from southern Italy. Since they left a nation that had been unified only in 1871, most still saw themselves not as Italians but as citizens of a certain town or district.

In the Italy they left, these immigrants had relied on their families for everything, and few had traveled beyond their villages. They arrived here unaware of the value of self-help societies, papers, or banks. However, once here, Italian Americans found they could accomplish little unless they united with people from other villages and built new institutions. Italian nationality flowered in the New World.

Italian immigrants arrive at Ellis Island filled with hope but unsure of the future.

The newcomers from Italy crowded into New York City ghetto neighborhoods. Families from their homeland districts helped the recent arrivals find jobs and homes. But families alone, they found, could not solve the new problems they faced.

Self-help organizations began to grow and to assume importance among Italian Americans. In Manhattan, by 1905, Italian immigrants and their children supported the Sons of Italy and 150 other mutual benefit societies.

At first these groups were organized by regions of Italy. But soon any Italian American who paid the 25 to 40 cents a month dues could join. By 1921, the Sons of Italy had 887 clubs and boasted 125,000 members from Brooklyn to Oregon. Using the dues of members, the clubs paid for funerals, illness, or hospital stays.

Italian immigrants at first often depended on the labor boss, or *padrone*, for jobs. He brought together men seeking work and employers who hired laborers. Though he may have arrived only a few years earlier, the *padrone* spoke Italian and English, knew where work could be found, and claimed a familiarity with American ways. He was not always trustworthy.

For a commission of $1 to $15, the *padrone* hired laborers, sent them to a nearby construction site, or shipped them to an employer hundreds of miles away. The *padrone* doled out wages, acted as banker, supplied immigrants with room and board, and wrote letters home. Many had a reputation for taking more than they gave and for squeezing what they could from recent arrivals.

Some *padrones* specialized in hiring men for highly dangerous work, or as strikebreakers. But this began to change as Italian Americans increasingly found a home in U.S. trade unions. As early as 1903, the International Hod Carriers and Building Laborers Union, reflecting its membership, issued its journal in Italian, German, and English. By 1908, Domenico d'Alessandro had become the union's president, and he held that position until his death in 1926. Italian Americans, such as Anzuino Marimpietri, helped found the Amalgamated Clothing Workers Union, of which Marimpietri became a vice president. Luigi Antonini was another Italian immigrant who played a major role in organizing the International Ladies Garment Workers Union.

At the turn of the century, Italian American women began to enter the labor market in large numbers. By 1910, not Jewish Americans but Italian Americans had become the largest proportion of women in the New York City garment industry. They also made up 72 percent of the employed workers in the artificial flower industry, and many young girls and women with children worked

These young immigrants were photographed in the factory they worked in for ten or more hours a day, six days a week. "None could read or write their own names," said Lewis Hine, who photographed the Italian boys.

at home. By 1919, in New York City, nine of every ten Italian girls and women over age 14 worked for wages.

Because their pay was very low and because Italian Americans had many children, parents encouraged their children to take jobs rather than stay in school. Sons and daughters were expected to work and turn their wages over to their father as the head of the family. At first, few children objected, but America was a new country.

The simple act of sons and daughters independently working for wages created stress in Italian American families. In Italy fathers had ruled supreme. But here teens began to resent handing over their hard-earned paycheck to their fathers. Even young women were no longer content to obey their fathers and surrender their wages.

A new generation born in the United States spoke English and understood American ways better than their mothers and fathers. The father of the house slowly but wisely learned to listen to the advice and words of his "Americanized" sons and daughters. A gulf often developed between adults and children as parents read Italian American papers and talked of the old country and their children read American papers, followed current trends, and said they were tired of hearing about village life in Italy.

A new generation of young men (and then young women) began a serious social revolution. The young no longer wanted parents to chose their marriage partners. Increasingly, the young dated and married non-Italians and even non-Catholics. Many of those who did marry Italian Americans rejected the idea of large families. The new generation also argued with parents and clergymen. Many of the young wanted to move away from the old neighborhood.

CHAPTER 11

INTO THE TWENTIETH CENTURY

The decades that ended the 19th century and began the 20th century were marked by change and adjustment. Immigrants made strides in the nation's economic, cultural, and political life. Members of the New Immigration, such as Italian Americans, had begun to climb the ladders of political success. In 1870 Carlo Rapollo, an Italian American, was elected to New York's Court of Appeals and served until his death in 1887. In 1895 Anthony Caminetti was elected to Congress. In 1900 Andrew Longino was the elected governor of Mississippi.

Blacks in the South and Mexican Americans in the Southwest became victims of lynch mobs. Black Representative Thomas E. Miller complained to Congress that "the first and dearest right" of the African American farmer "is his right to know that the man who lynches him will not the next day be elected by the state to a high and honorable trust." By 1900, many people of color had been driven from the polling booth and the levers of power. The justice and political systems North and South were white systems.

In 1890 Native Americans under Wovoka, a Paiute Indian, began a religious revival among the Sioux and other Plains nations. A special dance and chant, Wovoka predicted, would lead to their salvation, restore their dead warriors, and destroy their white enemies. His Ghost Dance religion captured the imagination of the Sioux Chief Big Foot and many other Sioux.

In 1890 Big Foot led 120 men and 230 women and children off reservation land to perform Ghost Dance ceremonies. Then, they headed back to the Pine Ridge Reservation in

The Ghost Dance ceremony.

47

Sioux Chief Big Foot, slain at Wounded Knee, lay frozen in the snow.

North Dakota. At Wounded Knee, South Dakota, the Ghost Dancers were surrounded by Colonel James Forsyth's 7th Cavalry. The Sioux went to sleep under his trained carbines and four Hotchkiss cannons.

In the morning there was a scuffle in the Sioux camp and then a rifle shot. The 7th Cavalry opened fire on the camp, and 300 Sioux died. "We tried to run," said one, "but they shot us like we were buffalo." The Secretary of War claimed that Forsyth had repelled an assault and awarded 18 cavalrymen the Congressional Medal of Honor. Any further Native American military resistance to United States domination virtually died that morning at Wounded Knee.

Bigotry also struck at immigrants. In 1890, 11 Italian Americans were jailed in New Orleans to await trial for murder. A white mob forced its way into their cells and murdered them. The next year Jewish American workers were chased from a New Jersey factory. In 1893 mobs gutted Jewish American homes in Mississippi, and in Louisiana mobs drove some Jewish storekeepers from the state.

One of the fastest-growing organizations of the 1890s was the

American Pastime

By the 1870s, baseball had become a popular sport in America. At first almost two dozen African Americans played on minor league teams. But in 1888, after one white manager strongly objected to integrated teams, they were barred from the game.

Two of the players who lost their minor league jobs in 1888 were Sol White and Weldon Walker. Walker wrote a letter to the league president: "The rule that you have passed is a public disgrace! It casts derision on... the voice of the people, which says that all men are equal."

But by the 1890s segregation ruled American baseball. African American team owners and managers then formed their own leagues, wrote their own schedules, and hired their own players. Black men of major league caliber received a yearly salary of $466, compared to $2000 by white major leaguers and $571 by white minor leaguers. Sol White wrote: "In no other profession has the color line been drawn more rigidly than in baseball." ■

American Protective Association (APA). It blamed the world's evils on Catholicism, the pope, and "aliens." APA books and pamphlets claimed Catholic priests had plotted Lincoln's assassination and were planning to arm "Irish Catholics in the great cities" and seize the U.S. government. In 1893 APA leaders announced Catholics planned a massacre of Protestants. When no violence took place, the APA claimed its warning had saved many people from death.

By 1894, the APA was issuing 70 weekly publications. These demanded Congress limit immigration and grant the vote only to people who spoke English and had lived in the U.S. for seven years.

By 1896, the APA was in decline. Its speakers were pelted with eggs in New York. In Savannah, Georgia, they had to be rescued from a mob by the militia. The 100 congressmen and senators the APA claimed as members could not be found to speak out in its defense. Then the APA endorsed William McKinley for president. Because McKinley had some Catholic friends, the group split over the endorsement and finally died out.

At the turn of the century, the United States was also calling itself a liberator. In 1898 the United States had entered the Spanish-American War to free Cuba from Spain. After a swift victory, the United States gained control of Cuba and of Spain's other colonies in the Caribbean and Pacific.

Emilio Aguinaldo. To Filipinos he was a liberator, but to the U. S. government he was an enemy.

Important leaders, such as Carl Schurz and Mark Twain, opposed the control of distant colonies. If the United States could fight to save Cuba, African Americans asked, why could it not save the 101 black citizens who had died that year at the hands of lynch mobs? When a black delegation asked President McKinley to prosecute South Carolina whites who had slain an African American postmaster and killed members of his family, he did nothing.

In the war with Spain, black soldiers helped bring victory. The black 10th Cavalry reached San Juan Hill in Cuba ahead of Teddy Roosevelt and his famous "Rough Riders."

In the Philippines, the U.S. Army first assisted Filipino nationalist leader Emilio Aguinaldo and his guerrilla troops in their fight for liberation. But U.S. troops then became an army of occupation and battled

Aguinaldo's men for three years. Most African Americans favored Aguinaldo's resistance to U.S. rule, and one black paper wrote sarcastically, "Maybe the Filipinos have caught wind of the way Indians and Negroes have been Christianized and civilized."

The United States had become an imperialist nation controlling resources in its Caribbean and Pacific possessions. Americans were, said Senator Albert Beveridge, "God's chosen people. The mission of our race," he said, is "trustee, under God, of the civilization of the world." The United States would, he said, "administer government among savages."

After a few years, Cuba became an independent nation, but Puerto Rico, Guam, Wake Island, and the Philippines remained within America's empire. They received new sewage systems that prevented disease, and they also received modern educational systems. But officials were sent from Washington to manage the affairs of these islands, and they brought with them racial discrimination and segregation to the new island colonies. Missionaries arrived to convert people to Christianity.

The new colonial empire opened the doors to people who wished to seek jobs on the U.S. mainland. Citizens of Puerto Rico and the Philippines began to visit the United States, and some stayed. When the Virgin Islands were purchased from Denmark in 1917, citizens of these islands also began to arrive in the United States. Newcomers from other islands began to emigrate, too.

Defeating Yellow Fever

Dr. Juan Carlos Finlay was born in Cuba to parents who had come from Scotland and France. He had studied medicine in Philadelphia and by 1881, was on his way to identifying the type of mosquito in Cuba that carried yellow fever. After the Spanish-American War, Dr. Finlay's lonely quest was joined by American Major Walter Reed. In experiments on army volunteers, the two men proved Finlay's claim that the disease was spread by mosquitoes. Reed ordered the destruction of the mosquitoes' swamp homes, and yellow fever died out. Ending this disease saved many lives and made possible the building of the Panama Canal. From 1902 to 1909, Dr. Finlay served as Cuba's chief health officer. ∎

CHAPTER 12

PROGRESS THROUGH INVENTIVE GENIUS

In the early part of the 20th century, America was transformed from a nation of small farms into a modern industrial giant with a large part of most of its population living in large cities. This enormous change and growth was sparked in many ways by the inventive genius of immigrants and minorities.

Alexander Graham Bell, born in Scotland in 1847, migrated to Canada in 1870 and then to America. Fascinated by speech, he developed a phonetic alphabet of the Mohawk language and trained teachers of the deaf.

On March 10, 1876, Bell spoke the words "Mr. Watson, come here. I want you" into a contraption of wires and was heard by his assistant in another room. The telephone was born, and in 1877 the Bell Telephone Company was formed.

Alexander Graham Bell demonstrates an invention in 1877.

In 1886 Bell became a naturalized American citizen. He continued his career as an educator of the deaf, and he continued to perfect his telephones.

The rapid production of daily papers was made easier in 1884 when Ottmar Mergenthaler, a German immigrant, invented a machine that set a line of type in seconds. Before this invention, each letter had to be set by hand, and the process took hours. Communication was also helped when John Gregg arrived from

Edison invented this machine to record stock prices.

Ireland in 1893 with his system of shorthand writing. A collection of longhand strokes, Gregg's system could be easily read by anyone who memorized his simple code.

Although he never had a formal education, Thomas Edison, born in 1847 to immigrants from Scotland, became one of the world's greatest inventors. Edison was taken out of a New Jersey school because he was a slow learner and was educated at home by his mother. He invented an electrographic vote tabulator, a phonograph, an incandescent electric light, and a movie projector. Among his more than a thousand inventions are the mimeograph, the storage battery, and the electric locomotive.

Michael Pupin, who arrived in the United States in 1874 from Hungary, taught electromechanics and mathematical physics at Columbia University from 1889 to 1931. As an inventor, Pupin devised ways of combining telephone and telegraph communications over long distances. In 1896 he was the first American to produce an X-ray photograph, and he discovered secondary X-ray radiation. In 1923 his autobiography, *From Immigrant to Inventor*, won a Pulitzer Prize.

In 1898 Irish immigrant John Holland completed a project he had labored on for decades: a submarine. His underwater craft was 53 feet 10 inches long and 10 feet 7 inches wide and was driven by a 50-horsepower engine operating on a storage battery.

Jan Matzeliger's new invention revolutionized the shoe industry.

Jan Matzeliger's device revolutionized shoe manufacturing. Born in Dutch Guiana to an African mother and a Dutch father, he took a job in a Lynn, Massachusetts, shoe factory. In 1883 he invented a lasting machine that virtually manufactured an entire shoe. It increased worker productivity 700 percent and made Matzeliger's hometown of Lynn the shoe capital of the world.

People from many other foreign lands also aided American industrial growth in the early years of the new century, some soon after their arrival. Akiba Horowitz came from Russia in 1890 and changed his name to Conrad Hubert. After jobs as a chef and as a salesman for the Lionel Train Company, in 1902 he developed and patented the flashlight. He organized and then sold the Eveready Company.

In 1907 a Jewish American doctor, Albert Michaelson, earned the Nobel Prize for his measuring instruments for the human eye. In 1909 Leo Baekelandt, a research chemist from Belgium, created modern plastic and brought about a plastic revolution, and in 1913 Gideon Sundback, a Swedish American, determined that shirts and blouses had to be made easier to open and close, invented the zipper. In 1914 Mary Phelps Jacob, a woman of Scottish and Irish American parents, patented the bra. It revolutionized women's styles and basic concepts of feminine beauty.

Hideyo Naguchi, a Japanese immigrant who arrived in 1899, became the first person to develop a test to diagnose syphilis. He also developed new ways of identifying and studying yellow fever and other diseases.

John Larson, who was born in Canada in 1892, graduated from Boston University in 1914 and received his doctoral degree in psychiatry in 1920 at the University of California. During his undergraduate studies, Larson came to believe that lying can be detected because it involves a deliberate or calculated effort, but telling the truth does not. He aimed to discover a way of measuring the kind of human effort involved in lying.

In 1921 Dr. Larson invented the "lie detector," or polygraph. It worked on the principle that fear of being caught in a lie pushes adrenalin through the body. This, he proved, can be measured scientifically through testing for pulse, breathing rates, blood pressure, and perspiration. Though not a foolproof device, his lie detector became a giant step in criminal investigation.

In 1923 Jacob Schick, son of a Bavarian immigrant, found himself in Alaska. It was 40 degrees below freezing, and there was no hot water. How satisfying, he thought, it would be to shave each morning without having to use cold water. He invented the electric razor.

African Americans were able to contribute hundreds of useful inventions in the decades following emancipation. George Washington Carver, born a Missouri slave in 1860, began to unlock the mysteries of ordinary southern crops. At Tuskegee Institute, Carver proved that planting peanuts, clover, or peas renewed soil with valuable nitrates. When farmers planted too many peanuts, Carver came to their rescue. He also discovered 325 new products to be made from peanuts, including types of cheese, milk, soap, and ink.

One of Elijah McCoy's inventions made him "the real McCoy."

Carver was able to create 118 products from sweet potatoes ranging from synthetic rubber to tapioca. He found that pecans could be made to create 75 products. He also used cotton to make products ranging from rugs to road-paving blocks.

Elijah McCoy, the son of runaway slaves, was educated in Scotland. In 1872 he invented a lubricating cup that fed oil to machines while they were still in operation. For the first time it became possible to oil locomotives, ship engines, and factory machinery without stopping them. Some called his lubricating cup "the real McCoy." He also held patents on more than 50 other inventions.

Lewis H. Latimer, born to runaway slaves in Boston, served in the Union Navy during the Civil War. An authority in electrical engineering and in drafting patents, he was hired by inventors Alexander Graham Bell and Thomas Edison and helped prepare the drawings required by the patent office for Bell's telephone.

Lewis Latimer worked on many of Edison's inventions.

Latimer also invented an incandescent electric light. In 1884 he was among the few men that Edison considered members of his original team, his "Edison Pioneers." In 1890 Latimer wrote the first book to explain the use of the electric light. As Edison's patent expert and star witness, Latimer testified in many cases when Edison's patents were challenged by others.

Perhaps the most significant African American inventor of the early 20th century was Garrett A. Morgan, who in 1914 developed a gas mask. In 1916 he and his brother Frank tested it after an explosion in a tunnel 250 feet under Lake Erie set off poisonous gases and trapped 32 men. Garrett and Frank Morgan donned masks and repeatedly entered the tunnel to carry out men overcome with smoke. The Morgan mask was used by American soldiers in Europe during World War I. In 1923 Morgan made a device that forever brought order to city streets and became a necessity for life in the city — the traffic light.

Dr. Williams' Miracle

Dr. Daniel Hale Williams, born in Pennsylvania in 1856, was fifth in a family of seven children born to parents of European, African, and Native American lineage. Williams was fascinated by medicine, and in 1884 he graduated from Chicago Medical College.

Because he was an African American, Williams was not allowed to practice in hospitals, so in 1891 he opened Provident Hospital in Chicago with African American doctors and nurses.

In 1893 James Cornish, stabbed during a fight, was brought to the hospital. He was unconscious, losing blood, and with a one-inch-deep wound near his heart.

Williams and his team of six surgeons conducted the first successful operation on the human heart. Williams sewed up the wound, and Cornish left the hospital in 51 days and lived for another 50 years, dying in 1943. Williams had died 12 years earlier. ■

CHAPTER 13

IMMIGRANT LABOR AND THE UNIONS

As immigrants poured into cities, employers sought to turn this abundant source of labor to their benefit. Managers used the newcomers as a threat against any workers who formed unions or went on strike for better working conditions. By paying these immigrants less money, corporations used the newcomers as scabs, people who take the jobs of striking workers.

Immigrants did not want jobs as strikebreakers. They wanted the same wages as the workers they replaced. Sometimes they quit their jobs as scabs and joined with the strikers. In 1885 the New York Bureau of Labor reported that at first immigrants "were willing to work for very low wages, but after a few years residence they became sufficiently Americanized to strike."

By 1886, Chicago had become a center of union activity, and many unions were led by radical immigrants. Corporate managers had persuaded the police that unions were dangerous conspiracies and that strikes were efforts at revolution. With this encouragement, police had often battled strikers and fired into union picket lines.

To unite working men and women, labor leaders in Chicago in 1886 organized the world's first May Day parade. European immigrants and their sons and daughters marched alongside other whites and people of color. Banners called for an 8-hour day, higher wages, and strong unions through the united efforts of working people.

The city's newspapers and the police had predicted violence, but the first May Day celebration was peaceful. However, three days later the police killed three strikers near the McCormick reaper plant.

A protest meeting was called for in Haymarket Square. In German and English, radical labor leaders denounced police, violence, and inhuman working conditions. Some anarchist speakers used fiery words to decry corporate greed, the police, and governments.

Most of the leaders and much of the audience had left the square, and the meeting was about to end when police marched in formation toward the speaker's stand. Suddenly a bomb exploded. It fatally wounded seven police officers. The police fired wildly into the crowd, injuring many. The bomber was never found.

In the hysteria that followed the explosion, eight radical union leaders were arrested for a plot to murder the police though only one was present when the bomb exploded. Seven of the eight were immigrants — six from Germany and one from England. The other was Albert Parsons, a white labor agitator from Texas.

Newspapers called the eight accused workers "foreign savages." They were found guilty, four were executed, and four were jailed.

The American Federation of Labor (AFL) was shaped during the Haymarket trials by its founders, Jewish immigrants Samuel Gompers and Adolph Strasser. The AFL planned to pursue conservative goals and to build a practical, pure, and simple national union for skilled labor. It promoted no lofty or radical ideas or political reforms and denounced radicals as dangerous and un-American. Instead, AFL "business unionism" aimed to raise wages, shorten hours, and improve labor conditions for skilled workers.

In its early years the AFL enrolled some women, but Gompers and the AFL were not really committed to their recruitment and soon stopped making the effort. In Toledo, Terre Haute, and Chicago, the AFL organized women in special "federal unions." Mrs. Hannah Morgan united typists, dressmakers, clerks, and music teachers in Chicago's AFL Ladies Federal Labor Union No. 2702.

The Lattimer Massacre

In 1897 in Luzerne County, Pennsylvania, United Mine Workers of America, which had 10,000 members, called a strike. It was surprised to find that 150,000 answered its call — largely American Lithuanians, Poles, Slovaks, Hungarians, Austrians, and Italians, with a sprinkling of other nationalities. Originally management had imported the foreign workers in order to cut the wages of workers who wanted better conditions and wages.

Men in one mine dropped their tools and marched off to recruit other miners to join the stoppage. Then, Luzerne sheriff Martin issued an order against marching on the local highways.

On September 10th, 500 strikers left Hazleton to "call out" their buddies in the Lattimer mines five miles away. Martin had 100 men deputized to confront the strikers. Without warning, the lawmen opened fire. "The deputies kept shooting at the miners after they were scattered and were running away," reported an eyewitness. The toll was 19 miners dead and 35 wounded.

The "Lattimer Massacre" shocked the nation. It also taught miners about the need for unity and strong organization. In 1938 Lithuanian American writer Stasys Michelsonas told how this terrible experience helped the United Mine Workers grow. He pridefully added, "All of the Lithuanian coal miners joined." ∎

"My education is poor," said Morgan, who told how at age 11 she had to work 16 hours a day in a mill. Using dynamic organizing methods, she soon had unions of watchmakers, bookbinders, and 21 other locals or branches. Her biggest, Union No. 2702, sponsored the Illinois Women's Alliance to advocate women's suffrage and the protection of women and children at work.

Morgan's campaigns led to a strict enforcement of Illinois' Compulsory Education Law and to the building of more schools. In 1891 she exposed the dangerous work employers required of children as young as 5 or 6 years old.

At first Gompers also urged labor to unite across racial lines:

If we fail to organize and recognize the colored wage-workers, we cannot blame them very well if they turn against us. If we fail to make friends of them, the employing class won't be so shortsighted and play them against us.

In 1891 Gompers asked those unions that had banned people of color to change their rules. He helped a boilermakers' union that welcomed African Americans to join the AFL by gaining an AFL charter of permission. That July, Gompers picked African American George Norton as secretary of a St. Louis Marine Fireman's Union. As an AFL organizer, Norton successfully recruited a mixed horseshoer's local in segregated New Orleans.

In 1892 Norton's St. Louis union showed what labor solidarity could accomplish. The city's striking African American dockworkers were joined by white laborers. The two groups formed a huge parade, carried banners, and heard speakers of both races. The police fired at the strikers, and the company hired scabs, but the strikers remained unified and won their wage demands.

That November, a New Orleans dock dispute led to the first citywide strike in the United States. A total of 49 unions that included 25,000 skilled and unskilled men and women of both races struck. When employers offered contracts only to white workers, the union leaders turned down this divisive tactic. The strike tied up New Orleans, and Gompers welcomed its labor solidarity:

> Never in the history of the world was such an exhibition,
> where with all the prejudices existing against the black
> man, when the white wageworkers of New Orleans
> would sacrifice their means of livelihood to defend and
> protect their colored fellow workers. With one fell sweep
> the economic barrier of color was broken down.

The strikes in St. Louis and New Orleans had shown a path of unity AFL leaders might have pursued. But the AFL soon ended its efforts to cross racial lines or organize people of color.

In the 1890s, AFL officials still talked about labor solidarity, but they had stopped recruiting immigrants, women, and people of color. Gompers now allowed AFL unions to ban minorities and women.

Discrimination was built into the AFL plan of organization. Its unions charged high dues and initiation fees. New candidates had to be recommended by members. These practices effectively left minorities and women out in the cold. But the main barrier minorities faced was the AFL pledge to enroll only skilled craft workers. Denied training and skills, people of color, women, and immigrants were not considered skilled workers.

The early policies of the AFL kept millions from joining unions and weakened the labor union movement in the United States. This failure helped employers keep wages low, hours of work high, and benefits few. It also meant that workers who would not stand together in unions would find it hard to unite on Election Day.

Unions Teach the Immigrants

In 1905 investigator Carroll Wright reported to President Theodore Roosevelt how Chicago stockyard unions "were teaching the immigrant the nature of the American form of government."

The unions in the stockyards are controlled by the Irish, ably assisted by the Germans. As a Bohemian or a Pole learns the language and develops, he is elected business agent or other official. In the port butchers' union, for instance, there are about 1,800 members, 600 of whom are Irish, 600 German, 300 Poles, and 300 Lithuanians and Slavs. The union recently elected a Pole as president of the local. In their business meetings the motions made, resolutions read, and speeches delivered are usually interpreted in five languages, though in some locals only in three. All business, however, is transacted primarily in English, although any member may speak to any motion in the language he best understands, his words being rendered into English for the minutes of the meetings and into all the languages necessary for the information of members. It is here that the practical utility of learning English is first brought home forcefully to the immigrant.... ■

At times immigrant laborers were able to unite.

CHAPTER 14

THE JAPANESE

Until 1885, the only Japanese in the United States were a few college students and some Japanese bankers and businesspeople who had journeyed to America for commercial reasons. But by 1891, enough Japanese Americans had settled in Oakland, California, to open their own Methodist church. And there were enough Japanese in Seattle, Washington, to support Shiro Fujioka's paper, the *North American Times*.

Soon after the Chinese Exclusion Act in 1882 kept Chinese from entering the United States, thousands of Japanese began to seek work in America. From 1901 to 1910, 130,000 Japanese immigrants came to take menial jobs, mostly in California.

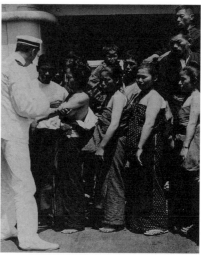

Japanese immigrants being vaccinated at sea, on the way to Hawaii.

Though they worked hard, kept to themselves, and had a low crime rate, prejudice against the newcomers rose with their increased immigration. In 1901 California governor Henry Gage said they were as much a "peril" as the Chinese. Some authorities believe that hatred toward the Japanese was almost inherited from the hatred against the Chinese who had been excluded.

The Japanese were able to survive animosity due in part to a sense of *on*, a great pride in and obligation to their families, villages, and country. A mixture of self-esteem and loyalty to others, *on* fortified the courage and faith of Japanese immigrants.

Not all arrivals from Japan were menial laborers. Dr. Hideyo Noguchi became a scientist at the Rockefeller Institute for Medical Research in 1904 and the first to identify syphilis in the nervous system of a patient. In 1901 a brilliant chemist, Dr. Jokichi Takamine, isolated pure adrenaline in the human body. In New York he founded the Nippon Club, which tried to improve relations between Japan and the United States.

Early in the 20th century these Japanese businessmen visited New York City.

Americans found a unique reason to dislike the Japanese — "their partial adoption of American customs." Japanese Americans became the first minority to be resented because of their ability to "be American." This, claimed their foes, gave them an unfair advantage when competing with white citizens in the workplace.

The press in California led the headline assault on the new "Yellow Peril." In February 1901, the widely read San Francisco *Chronicle* featured a front page series with the headline, "The Japanese Invasion, The Problem of the Hour."

Within days the California Legislature instructed the California members of Congress to ask for a law ending migration from Japan. By May, 67 organizations in San Francisco had already formed an Asiatic Exclusion League, and alarm and fear soared in 1905 when tiny Japan soundly defeated Russia in the Russo-Japanese War.

Both the Japanese government and its citizens on United States soil tried to calm these fears. After the 1906 San Francisco earthquake, Japan contributed more relief funds than all other nations combined. But some people preferred to blame the Japanese in California for problems following the earthquake. Two Japanese who investigated the disaster for the University of Tokyo were stoned and beaten by white mobs in San Francisco.

The most insulting blow came in 1907 when San Francisco said it would segregate its Japanese American schoolchildren. Japan's ambassador complained to President Theodore Roosevelt, and he dispatched a cabinet member to San Francisco to resolve the issue. Before Roosevelt's negotiator arrived, anti-Japanese riots had rocked the city.

The solution finally agreed upon was a "Gentlemen's

Labor Fights "Mongrels"

Samuel Gompers and other leaders of the AFL played a leading role in campaigns to deny Asians entrance to America. Gompers claimed credit for the laws ending emigration from China. Next, he called for laws to exclude Japanese, whom he called "perverse, ignorant, malicious... mongrels."

In Oxnard, California, in 1903, Japanese American sugar beet workers struck against starvation wages and inhuman conditions. By uniting with Mexican Americans, they won wage increases and improved working conditions. The two people of color formed a union, and J. M. Larraras, the Mexican American secretary of the union, applied for membership in the AFL. Gompers told Larraras he first had to expel his Japanese American members. Instead, Larraras wrote Gompers telling him how Japanese Americans began the union and stood by Mexican Americans when one was killed. Larraras wrote:

> In the past we have counseled, fought and lived on very short rations with our Japanese brothers, and toiled with them in the fields, and they have been uniformly kind and considerate. We would be false to them and to ourselves and to the cause of unionism if we now accepted privileges for ourselves which are not accorded to them. We are going to stand by men who stood by us in the long, hard fight which ended in victory over the enemy.... We will refuse any other kind of a charter except one which will wipe out race prejudices and recognize our fellow workers as being as good as ourselves.

Nevertheless, the union was refused an AFL charter. ■

Agreement" treaty signed by the two nations. Japan agreed to keep its laborers from the U.S. in return for an end to the segregation of Japanese American children in California schools. Japan further agreed to prohibit its citizens from entering America from Canada, Mexico, or Hawaii, and immigration fell from 10,000 a year to 2,500.

But resentment toward Japanese Americans continued. White anger did not differentiate between *Issei*, who were born in Japan, and *Nisei*, who are Japanese Americans born in the United States. Both groups became targets of violent white mobs in California.

Animosity toward Japanese Americans also took the form of exclusion from labor unions. AFL unions refused to enroll Japanese Americans and then called them "cheap" for working below union scales or for taking jobs of those on strike.

By 1908, 231 labor and other groups joined an Asiatic Exclusion League. By that year, more Japanese Americans left the United States than arrived from Japan. Still white bitterness continued.

By 1910, California legislators had proposed 27 bills to restrict the newcomers. Only intervention from the White House prevented passage of these bills. President William Howard Taft was trying to avoid an international incident.

The Japanese government repeatedly tried to see that its people were treated fairly in America. In 1912 as a goodwill gesture, Japan shipped valuable cherry trees to the United States.

In contrast to their treatment in the continental United States, Japanese citizens entered Hawaii, which was an American possession but not yet a state, without any incidents. By 1920, 48 percent of Hawaii's diverse population was of Japanese origin.

In 1913 California passed a law that denied a person of Japanese descent the right to own land or to lease it for longer than three years. Even when Japan became an ally of the United States during World War I, the law was kept on the books, and the media continued to spin tales of an enormous "Yellow Peril."

Meanwhile, Japanese American laborers produced most of California's strawberries and introduced a variety of new fruits and vegetables. They produced a tenth of the agricultural products of California. Everyone agreed that Japanese Americans knew how to utilize marginal land, develop irrigation systems, and drain marshy soil. However, whites saw this not as a benefit but as a menace.

Japanese Americans became lawyers, scholars, and teachers, and some Japanese American farmers were successful enough to buy their own land through their children's names. In San Francisco some Japanese American professionals formed the American Loyalty League to fight racial discrimination.

But white bitterness was unrelenting. Books, magazines, and papers with stories about the "Yellow Menace" sold well, and movies caricatured Japanese Americans as sinister and corrupt.

CHAPTER 15

THE KOREANS

In 1903 the first 121 Korean laborers landed in the American possession of Hawaii. Others followed, and Korean men and women were soon laboring in the sugarcane fields, men for $18 a month, women for less. A Korean who became a *luna*, or foreman, wrote:

> I was in charge of 250 workers — 200 men and 50 women. After receiving my assignment, I would take my group out to the fields and begin work at six. We worked 10 hours a day in the blazing sun and had only a half hour for lunch.... I had workers of all races in my group — Hawaiians, Filipinos, Puerto Ricans, Chinese, Japanese, Portuguese, and Koreans.... We would quit work at 4:30 and walk wearily back to the train that would take us back to camp. When we got back to camp, we ate, washed, and went directly to bed. During the harvest season, we worked seven days a week. But at other times of the year we had Sundays off.

About 7,000 Koreans settled in Hawaii in the early 1900s. There they found a strange and alien culture. Whites wore strange clothes, smoked cigarettes, and did not eat rice daily. "Don't you, even for fun," a Korean mother warned her son, "put on foreign clothes."

In 1905, after Japan defeated Russia, Japan seized Korea and ended emigration to the United States. After 1910, when Japan formally annexed Korea, 2,000 Koreans returned home from Hawaii to be with their families. Others decided to remain until their homeland was free.

Beginning in the 1890s, Koreans began to come to the United States as students. In 1903 three young immigrants, Hong Seung-ha, Ahn Jong-su, and Yun Byong-gu, formed a New People's Association to promote Korean unity and independence from Japan. A month later in San Francisco, Ahn Ch'ang-ho and six other students met in a restaurant to form the Friendship Society for Korean American students.

Koreans in Hawaii began to pour into San Francisco, and by 1910, they had issued more than a dozen religious and secular papers. That year one Korean immigrant and a future president of Korea, Syngman Rhee, published his book, *The Spirit of Independence*.

Korean American families tried to preserve their ancient heritage in food, dress, language, and customs. They cherished the elderly and children. They used chopsticks and wooden pillows. Many of the newcomers gathered each year to celebrate the emperor of Korea's birthday with singing, feasting, and drinking.

Korean American culture and religion began to grow. In 1906 San Francisco had a Korean Methodist church whose congregation met in a rented house. The following year it published the Korean Federation Church Bulletin. By 1928, the congregation had raised $18,000 and had constructed its own building.

Ancient mores held firm in Korean American families. The sexes were rigidly separated, even at festivals. Men requested brides from their homeland. Based on a woman's photograph, a man made his choice and paid for her passage to the United States. Well-dressed young women began to arrive from Korea and Hawaii.

Korean American families were large, with five to eight children. They celebrated the first birthday of a male but not of a female child. Parents tried to bring Korea's traditional wisdom to the young, but in the United States the public schools Americanized their children. Korean American communities were too small to sustain their own schools. Public school playmates and teachers were a potent force for assimilation that Korean-born parents could not match. An American-born generation showed little interest in a free Korea or in returning to a land they had never seen.

Some Korean Americans continued to support the liberation of Korea from Japanese rule. In 1909 in San Francisco, the Korean National Association was formed to promote independence. But disputes erupted among its leaders, and efforts to unite the Korean community in America largely failed.

Pak Yong-man, who arrived in San Francisco in 1905, began to advocate armed resistance against Japanese rule over Korea. In 1914 he began to give military training to 300 young Koreans in Hawaii.

More peaceful groups were started by women. In 1913 the Korean Women's Association (KWA) in Hawaii was formed with Maria Whang as its leader. It sought to promote the Korean language, education, and the provision of aid for the needy. It ordered a boycott of all Japanese products until the homeland was free.

Some Korean women formed other groups. In 1917 Yang Chehyon organized a Korean Women's Association in Sacramento, California, to boycott Japan and promote self-determination for Korea. In 1919 Korean American women in Sacramento and Los Angeles united to foster Korea's independence. In August 1919 Korean American women in California held a conference to unify their many efforts on behalf of their people in America and the ancestral homeland.

CHAPTER 16

FROM THE ARAB WORLD

People from the Arab world began to arrive in the United States in the late 19th century. Most of these early immigrants were Christian rather than Muslim, and only a few were women. By 1892, the first paper published in Arabic had appeared in New York City, and by 1907, it had competition from seven others. These periodicals printed news about the homelands, life in the United States, social notes, fiction, poetry, and literature. They urged new arrivals to learn English and adopt American ways.

Migration from Arab lands to the United States was 4,000 annually in 1898 and went up to 9,000 in 1913. Most of the newcomers were Christian men from Lebanon, which was at that time part of Syria. They landed with an average of $14. Illiteracy among these immigrants was 44 percent, lower than the average rate among most European immigrants. Soon Muslim Arabs also began to arrive in the United States.

By 1910, Christian Iraqis were entering America, and many sought out the Detroit area for jobs and homes. Women made up 47 percent of these arrivals. Some sailed here to join their husbands or to find husbands. Others came to find work and success on their own. Sumayeh Attujeh, educated at an American school in Tripoli, arrived here in 1912 to study medicine. An expert on Islamic civilization, she lectured before U.S. audiences for 15 years.

Syrian Americans kept particularly strong bonds with relatives and the homeland and sent home more money than any other immigrant group. Three out of every four Syrian immigrants eventually decided to make the United States their home.

These newcomers were often drawn to jobs that involved selling goods and services. Before 1914, nine out of ten Arab men and women arrivals took jobs as peddlers. In 1908 a Syrian Business Directory listed Arab enterprises in almost every state.

Despite the hardships and uncertainties of the road, especially

A Syrian Armenian vendor sells cool drinks in New York City.

A Turkish American street peddler in 1898.

for women, selling goods for a living fostered Syrian American self-reliance. For those who arrived with little cash and little knowledge of English, selling had many attractions. It required little training, little money for investment, and merely a knowledge of basic English. Yet selling yielded higher pay than work in mines and mills.

Arab American peddling networks often had up to 60 men and women working together, often selling products from the Arab lands. With New York as their center, recently arrived Arabs were fed into these sales networks. Though largely Christian Lebanese, these women and men were called Syrians since that was the nation from which they had sailed.

Horses, wagons, and then cars carried these peddlers and their linens, laces, and rugs across the American countryside. Men and women were on the road weeks at a time selling their dry goods. Success came slowly, but financial failures were few.

Door-to-door selling had unanticipated results for peddlers. It helped improve the newcomer's knowledge of English, and it introduced the peddlers to other Americans and to the American value system. Many who had planned to return home after their success decided instead to settle in the United States.

Some former Arab peasants became heads of or executives in successful businesses in the United States. Lebanese immigrant Michael Shadid arrived as a student in 1890. To complete his medical education, he worked as a door-to-door peddler and saved $5,000. Later, as a well-known doctor, Shadid founded the Community Hospital in Elk City, Oklahoma, America's first cooperative and low-cost medical institution. In his *Crusading Doctor*, Shadid told the hospital's fascinating story.

From Lebanon to America

Khalil Gibran was 13 years old when he arrived in Boston from Lebanon in 1895 with his mother, two sisters, and brother. Gibran became a painter, and his paintings began to draw public attention. By the time he was 21 years old, Gibran's paintings had received widespread acclaim. Many of his portraits are in famous galleries.

By 1908, Gibran also had published three books. In addition, he wrote short stories and poetry in Arabic for the immigrant community. One story began dramatically, "I am Lebanese and I'm proud of that."

Gibran's stories won him literary fame. News of his success reached the Muslim world he had left behind.

In 1919 Gibran began to write in English for his American readers, and his fame grew. His book *The Prophet*, published in 1923, is a collection of his poems on love, beauty, and death, and became an American best-seller. He described himself as "Syrian in my desires, Lebanese in my feelings." When he died in 1931, Gibran was buried, according to his wishes, in the Lebanese village of his birth, Basharri. ■

A Syrian dance was one way of remaining close to one's cultural roots.

For followers of Islam, pursuing traditional religious rituals in America was difficult, if not impossible. In a Christian nation Muslims struggled to observe Friday as the Sabbath, pray five times a day, and fast during their important Ramadan period.

In Ross, North Dakota, a Muslim settlement that was started around 1900 took a quarter of a century to build a mosque. By then, many worshippers felt they had lost their Arab identity and language. Some residents had adopted Christian names, and they had seen their children be assimilated into American culture, marry non-Muslims, and move away.

After 1910, a trend toward urban work began as Muslim Americans took jobs in Chicago, Toledo, and in industrial cities in Michigan. Few Arab Americans sought farm work. In the quarter century that ended in 1930 nine out of ten Syrian Americans settled in urban centers — more than 7,000 in New York City, more than 5,500 in Detroit, and more than 3,000 in Boston.

From their arrival, Arabs Americans, Christian or Muslim, experienced little discrimination. Their numbers were small, and their population centers were inconspicuous or seen as quaint.

CHAPTER 17

IMMIGRANTS FROM INDIA

In 1902 a severe four-year drought drove 7,000 farm workers from the Punjab region of India to California. These Indians were Sikhs, members of a religion that had begun centuries earlier. They arrived at the height of American animosity toward other Asians. Sikhs also stirred white hatred because they wore turbans, had dark skins, and came from a radically different culture. Some whites derisively called Sikhs "rag heads."

A few of the immigrants were Hindus, and most were Caucasians. Many came with valuable agricultural skills, and that helped them easily find jobs in California's vineyards.

Those immigrants from the Punjab were often younger sons sent by fathers to earn the cash to pay family debts in India. Others arrived to make enough money to buy land in the Punjab. Some of these migrants had learned English while serving as soldiers during the British occupation of India.

Many Indians first landed in British Columbia, Canada, where they had taken railroad jobs. Some Sikhs then took lumbering jobs in America's Washington State but met mounting racial fury there. In 1907 about 1,000 were driven from jobs near the Washington towns of Bellingham and Everett.

Hindu immigrants worked hard in America.

When Canada excluded East Indian migrants the next year, United States railroad builders convinced steamship lines to bring Sikh laborers to California. During the next two years, thousands of Sikhs worked for the Western Pacific Railroad.

They next took winter work in Yuba City, Stockton, and El Centro, California, work which once had been done by Mexican

Americans and Japanese Americans. Sikhs also labored on farms in California's Sacramento, San Joaquin, and Imperial valleys.

Some Indian students worked in hospitals and laundries to pay for their college tuition, and they also took agricultural jobs during the summer. These Sikh students ran their own boardinghouses, since they were banned from fraternities and often excluded from restaurants and hotels. Their boardinghouses became their homes and debating and social centers. Refugees from British rule or advocates of Indian independence formed a small part of India's emigrants.

A student from Bengal, India, Taraknath Das, born in 1884, attended the University of Washington between 1908 and 1910 and published the *Free Hindustan*. In 1914 he joined with Har Dayal (born in 1887) to form the Ghadar Party to unite Muslim, Sikh, and Hindu immigrants from India. In several languages their paper, *Ghadar*, promoted self-determination for India.

Americans from India faced an uphill battle for U.S. citizenship. The 1790 U.S. Naturalization Act stated that only "free whites" could gain citizenship. In 1906 this law was used to deny Asians U.S. citizenship on the basis of skin color. In 1910 and 1913 federal courts ruled that Indian Caucasians were eligible for U.S. citizenship, and about a hundred became citizens. Then, in 1923, the U.S. Supreme Court reversed this ruling, and 50 Indian Americans suddenly found their citizenship was again revoked.

Dr. Sakharam Ganesh Pandit, who arrived from India in 1906, earned a law degree at the University of Chicago and became a U.S. citizen in 1914. He became a California attorney and a noted college lecturer. When his citizenship was revoked by the 1923 ruling, he and his wife carried their case all the way to the U.S. Supreme Court and finally regained their full citizenship rights.

Protracted and frustrating legal battles against bigotry led many Indians to pack up and leave the United States. Some found another way of gaining citizenship — by marrying women who were citizens. Marriage to a citizen made a foreigner eligible for U.S. citizenship. In their determination to become American citizens, fully half of single male Indian farm workers married Mexican American women. By the time of World War I, U.S. federal law banned all further immigration by Asians.

FORMATION OF THE IWW

New immigrants, people of color, and women often found it hard to rise above the lowest salary levels paid for unskilled and skilled work in America. For every dollar paid an American-born laborer, arrivals from Italy received 84 cents, Hungarians 68 cents, and others from eastern and southern Europe as little as 54 cents. People of color and women were paid even less.

Only 2 million people, almost entirely skilled white men, were members of unions. The largest union, the AFL, generally excluded minorities.

Finally, in 1905, a new union, the International Workers of the World (IWW), appeared to challenge the traditional exclusion of minorities, women, and the unskilled from the unions. The Industrial Workers of the World accepted all workers regardless of skill, sex, or race.

The IWW's leader, "Big Bill" Haywood, had been born in 1869 to Mormon parents in Utah, and his ancestors included Native Americans. He opened the first IWW convention in Chicago with the words:

"Big Bill" Haywood (center, in black derby) leading an IWW march.

It does not make a bit of difference whether he is a Negro or a white man. It does not make a difference whether he is American or foreigner.... When we get the unorganized and unskilled laborer into this organization, the skilled worker will of necessity come here for his own protection.

Haywood and the IWW also called for the overthrow of capitalism and its replacement with a socialist state in which the industries were run by a government dominated by working men and women.

The IWW founding convention drew a number of women and minorities. "Mother" Mary Jones, an Irish American from Canada, attended the convention, as did Lucy Parsons, a woman of color. Both women were already famous labor agitators. And the famous labor leader Eugene Debs was there. Debs was the son of Alsatian immigrants and had been the Socialist Party's candidate for president since 1900. An American Irish Catholic priest, Thomas Hagerty, and William Trautman, a German immigrant and editor of the United Brewery Workers Union publication *Brauer Zeitung*, also took a prominent part in the first IWW convention.

IWW leaders mobilized women and children in strikes against many corporations.

The IWW's espousal of socialism and its reliance on strikes rather than arbitration to settle labor disputes did not appeal to those women and minorities who sought a comfortable place in the middle class rather than strife. The Wobblies, as the IWW members were called, terrified business leaders and politicians.

The Women of the IWW

The AFL insisted that women were only temporarily in the labor market and therefore could not be unionized. Wobblies recruited women and demonstrated that the AFL words were merely an excuse not to unionize working women.

In IWW unions, women were promised equality and were made executive officers. Often women Wobblies fended off attacks on their picket lines or fought for men on strike.

In McKees Rocks, Pennsylvania, in 1909 the steel companies hired men from 16 different nationalities including Hungarians, Turks, Slovaks, Swiss, and Romanians. When the men struck, their families were evicted from company homes. But wives and daughters, in a spontaneous revolt, halted the evictions. To the men they shouted, "Kill the Cossacks! Crush them! If you are afraid, go home to the children and leave the work to us!"

The next year in an Indiana steel factory, 20 ethnic groups united to fight a pay cut. "Hundreds of women from the foreign settlement," reported the *Indianapolis Star*, "armed with brooms, clubs, stove pokers, rolling pins, and other kitchen utensils," clashed with police at the plant. One woman was slain and 12 were arrested. Some 1,500 workers assembled, and each knelt to swear an oath before a crucifix not to return to work until they had won. In three days they were victorious.

During a 1912 lumber strike in the state of Washington, 25 wives of Finnish Americans, Greek Americans, and others confronted scabs at Slade's Mill. A Seattle newspaper described the scene:

> The mill hose was turned on the women, and they were drenched. Several of the women had babies in carriages with them.... The women later marched in a body to the city hall and demanded protection for themselves.

"Every morning women have appeared at the mills with baby buggies," reported an eyewitness, "and every morning the mill hose has been turned on them." The women finally won the strike.

In a 1916 mine strike at Aurora, Illinois, wives of many ethnic groups, with their baby carriages, marched 75 miles to call out workers in a dozen languages. Women and children paraded with signs that read, "We Are Human Beings" and "We Want Milk." A local paper called the women "more trouble than the men."

Mothers were thrown in jail with their infants and children. Although families ran out of food, and the strike collapsed, mine owners had learned a lesson and announced two salary increases. ■

The leading organizers of the IWW reflected the union's mix of men and women of all races. African American Ben Fletcher, born in 1890, had helped organize the powerful Philadelphia Marine Transport Workers' Local 3. By 1916, his integrated longshore union of 3,000 controlled the docks of Philadelphia, and Blacks and whites rotated as the union's leaders. When he died in 1949, a Wobbly comrade eulogized Fletcher with this poem:

> Rest, rest old fighter rest,
> Your noble deeds by memory blest,
> Inspire us all in Freedom's quest,
> Rest, old fighter, rest.

Frank Little, born in 1879 to a Cherokee mother and Quaker father, became an IWW organizer in 1906. Little, ready to enter any labor struggle, soon bore the marks of beatings and arrests. In 1917 Little, suffering from rheumatism and walking with crutches because of a broken leg, rushed off to help striking miners in Butte, Montana. The night after he made a prostrike speech, six men broke into his room, and seized and killed him. The murderers were never brought to trial.

Joe Hill was an organizer who set the Wobblies' message to music. Born in Sweden in 1879 as Joe Hagglund, in 1902 he migrated to the United States, and in 1910 he joined the IWW as "Joe Hill." He traveled across country composing songs from familiar tunes and adding his own lyrics. His verses told working men and women why the Wobblies were their friends, why strikes were necessary, and why the rich were so selfish and their rule had to be overthrown.

In Salt Lake City in 1914, Hill was arrested for murder. In a climate of fear, Hill was convicted without evidence and sentenced to death. The Swedish ambassador asked the governor of Utah to commute Hill's sentence, and protests came from as far away as Germany, but in 1915 Hill was shot by a Utah firing squad.

The young Wobbly left behind the most famous message in labor history. Facing death, he wrote to Bill Haywood and said:

> Good-bye Bill. I will die like a true blue rebel. Don't waste time in mourning. Organize.

One of Hill's songs, "The Rebel Girl," celebrated the dynamic young organizer Elizabeth Gurley Flynn, who was born in poverty in 1890 to Irish immigrants. At age 18 Flynn was described as a "slender girl, pretty and graceful, with a resonant voice and a fiery eloquence that attracted huge crowds." She was often arrested and spent time in jail for helping strikers, and she became one of the founders of the American Civil Liberties Union (ACLU).

There are women of many descriptions
In this queer world as every one knows
Some are living in beautiful mansions
And are wearing the finest of clothes
There are blue-blooded queens and princesses
Who have charms made of diamond and pearl
But the only and thoroughbred lady
Is the Rebel Girl.

That's the Rebel Girl, that's the Rebel Girl
To the Working class she's a precious pearl
She brings courage and pride and joy
To the fighting Rebel Boy
We have girls before but we need some more
In the Industrial Workers of the World.
For it's great to fight for freedom
With a Rebel Girl.

—words and music by Joe Hill, 1905

In strike after strike Wobbly organizers tried to rally women, immigrants, and minorities to their "one big union." In Lawrence, Massachusetts, in 1913, the Wobbly strike committee represented 27 nationalities. Journalist Ray Stannard Baker wrote "It was the first strike I ever saw which sang." At meetings, Baker heard and saw "the strange, sudden fire of mingled nationalities." Despite police attacks on women pickets and their children, the strikers won large pay increases.

In Paterson, New Jersey, that same year, Haywood and Flynn helped striking women and men silk workers of many ethnic groups. Forbidden to meet in Paterson, thousands of singing workers marched to Haledon, New Jersey, for their rallies. A journalist wrote:

Joe Hill dedicated this song to Elizabeth Gurley Flynn.

> The feeling of comradeship between all the workers was beautiful to see; all nationalities stood side by side in perfect order and listened to the counsel of the leaders. Here and there someone would be translating the speech as it went along for the benefit of those who could not understand it.

When mill owners declared "flag day" to protest against "the foreign" IWW leadership, the union had an answer. Strikers wore small flags and the words, "We wove the flag; we dyed the flag; we live under the flag; but we won't scab under the flag!"

After 14 weeks, desperate men and women went back to work. Wobbly leaders explained their defeat in Paterson as: "Hun-ger. Nothing else. Five months' hunger."

Late in 1913 the IWW aided 14,000 striking Colorado miners. The Colorado Fuel and Iron Company ruled southern Colorado and hired a mixture of American Germans, Turks, Greeks, Swedes, Slavs, Montenegrins, Mexicans, Poles, French, Finns, Canadians, Hungarians, Austrians, Italians, and Russians.

GIVE US
A LIVING WAGE
NOT CHARITY

The IWW mobilized children in a huge pageant to win support during the 1913 Paterson strike.

Journalist John Reed found that mine owners had carefully studied which ethnic groups might be "most patient under oppression and deliberately imported ignorant foreigners to work the mines." Owners mixed men of "different languages, who would not be able to organize."

But once this work force went on strike, it remained united. Officials evicted the striking workers from their homes, and 9,000 strikers set up tent colonies. Reed described the largest at Ludlow:

There were more than 1,200 people, divided into 21 nationalities, undergoing the marvelous experience of learning that all men are alike. When they had been living together for two weeks, the petty race prejudices and misunderstandings that had been fostered between them by the coal companies for so many years began to break down. Americans began to find out that Slavs and Italians and Poles were as kindhearted, as cheerful, as loving and brave as they were. The women called upon one another, boasting about their babies and their men, bringing one another little delicacies when they were sick. The men played cards and baseball together.

In January 1914 the mine owners, assisted by the Colorado State Militia, launched a reign of terror against the strikers. One April morning 20 state militia machine guns raked the Ludlow tent colony. Screaming mothers dragged their children under their tents or ran for the hills. Reported an eyewitness,

The soldiers and mine guards tried to kill everybody; anything they saw move, even a dog, they shot at.

This became known in American history as "the Ludlow Massacre."

CHAPTER 19

ACHIEVING THE AMERICAN DREAM

During the years of the new immigration, some members of minorities reached success on various personal levels. They demonstrated it was possible to achieve the American dream.

John Peter Altgeld was born in Germany in 1847. When he was 3 months old, his parents took him to the United States. He lived and worked in Ohio, had little time for school, and became a Union soldier in the Civil War. After the war, he studied law in Savannah, Missouri, and in 1870 he was admitted to the bar. The next year he was appointed city attorney.

Altgeld wrote a book titled *Our Penal System and Its Victims* to argue that poverty produced criminals, and jails failed to reform them. For five years he served as a judge on the Illinois Superior Court. He insisted that the state had an obligation to protect the weak from the economically and politically powerful. He spoke out for the secret ballot, the 8-hour day, labor's right to strike, and other reforms.

Immigrant John Atgeld became a leading figure in the reform wing of the Democratic Party at the turn of the century.

In 1892 when Altgeld ran for governor of Illinois, his campaign speeches attacked the greed of rich corporations. After he was elected governor, Altgeld did things no other governor had ever done. He issued an official proclamation denouncing the lynching of a black man. And he not only pardoned three men who had been framed for the Haymarket bombing, but he also called their trial an outrage based on evidence invented by police and accepted by a biased judge. Newspapers called Altgeld an anarchist and Communist, but journalist Nelly Bly interviewed Altgeld and said "he is going to do as he thinks right every time, if the whole world stands still."

During the depression of 1893, which created widespread misery and joblessness, Governor Altgeld refused to let his troops break strikes as other governors had done. Most strike violence, he said, was promoted by bosses who demanded that officials intervene to break picket lines, wreck unions, and protect scabs.

In the nationwide Pullman strike Altgeld challenged President Grover Cleveland, a fellow Democrat, over how to handle the strike. Altgeld had kept Chicago calm, but Cleveland ordered U.S. troops into the city to break the strike. Altgeld charged the President had violated the Constitution and the principles of self-government. A president cannot send federal troops into a state without a governor's request.

The press called Altgeld a "lying, hypocritical, demagogical, sniveling Governor." One paper snarled that he did not have "an ounce of American blood in him."

Many now considered Altgeld a political corpse. But the governor continued to denounce the President and his illegal use of troops to crush the rail union and the strike. In 1896 it was Altgeld, not Cleveland, who shaped the Democratic platform and selected William Jennings Bryan as the presidential candidate. To defeat Bryan, the press again attacked Altgeld.

Meanwhile, the governor had rolled up an impressive record in Illinois. He had reformed the civil service system, prisons, and the courts. He had had the legislature pass laws that limited child labor and sweatshops, required state inspection of factories, and mandated an 8-hour day for women. And he had provided financial aid to the University of Illinois and built many parks in poor neighborhoods.

Altgeld was defeated as governor in 1896 and left office in poor health though he was only 49 years old. In 1900 he was still a powerful enough force in the Democratic Party to write its platform. On the morning of his death in 1902, Altgeld defended a taxi union in court, and in the afternoon he gave a lecture on justice.

Amadeo Pietro Giannini was born in San Jose, California, in 1870. His father had come to America from Genoa, Italy. As a boy he watched in horror when his father was murdered by a neighbor.

His mother remarried a produce broker, and Giannini, in his early teens, joined his stepfather's firm. By the time he was 31, Giannini had made enough money in the company to retire.

Instead of retiring, however, Giannini, with help in 1904 from a Jewish friend named Hellman, opened a bank in San Francisco for immigrants. Italian immigrants, he knew, distrusted most bankers, so he made his institution unique, called it the "Bank of Italy," and advertised for customers in foreign-language papers.

In 1906 a devastating earthquake almost destroyed San Francisco. Giannini took $2 million in bank funds, climbed into a horse-drawn wagon, and sought out his depositors in streets filled with rubble. He handed cash to depositors and also lent funds to others in distress who could offer no security. To one man he said, "Your face is sufficient security." Another's calloused hands, he said, proved he was a "hard-working man. We need you to rebuild the city."

Giannini was the first to build bank branches on both the East and West coasts. His competitors called his innovations offensive — especially for someone who was not Anglo-Saxon. But Giannini welcomed originality. With his brother, Atillio, he was among the first bankers to lend funds to the new film industry and to its Jewish immigrant owners Marcus Loew, Lewis Selznick, Florenz Ziegfield, and the Warner brothers.

Sara Breedlove, as Madam C. J. Walker, became the first African American woman to earn a million dollars.

The Bank of Italy became the largest bank in the United States, and the Gianninis became very wealthy. They proudly renamed their institution the "Bank of America."

Sara Breedlove became the first American woman to earn a million dollars by her own labor. Born in 1867 to poor African American farmers in Louisiana, she was orphaned in childhood and raised by a married sister. At age 14 Sarah married, but four years later her husband died and left her a widow with a daughter. She left for St. Louis where she washed clothes for a living.

In 1905 Breedlove began working on a formula for straightening the hair of African American women and a cream for lightening their complexion. She moved to Denver, Colorado, where she married Charles Walker, a journalist. She also began to sell her products door to door, and her territory spread into the South and East. Mrs. Walker expanded her enterprise and trained sales agents. By 1910, she owned a manufacturing plant and business offices in Indianapolis and had 3,000 employees, mostly women.

The Choice of Exiles

The United States has always welcomed exiled visionaries and revolutionists. Many Puerto Rican nationalists who made New York City their refuge included Ramon Emeterio Betances (1827-1898), who organized Puerto Rico's first attempt to become a republic; independence fighter Eugenio Maria de Hostos (1839-1903); Santiago Iglesias (1872-1939), a founder of the Puerto Rican Socialist Party; and Luis Muñoz Rivera (1859-1916), who created the first effort at an autonomous government for Puerto Ricans in 1898 after the United States took over the island.

José Martí y Pérez, born in Cuba in 1853, had to flee his homeland at age 16. In 1881 he settled in Brooklyn, New York, and soon organized the Cuban Revolutionary party. He wrote two books that analyzed South American political issues and toured many Cuban American communities to rally both his black and his white followers to overthrow Spain's rule of the island. In 1895 he left his exile in the United States to join the Cuban revolution and died in battle.

James Connolly, born in Ireland in 1870, lived in the United States as a revolutionary exile from 1902 until he returned for Ireland's Easter Rebellion of 1916. In the United States he honed his radical ideas, tried to influence Irish Americans, and worked with U.S. labor leaders. As one of the leaders of Ireland's Easter Rebellion in 1916, Connolly was captured and executed by a British firing squad, but his death helped unite the Irish as never before.

Karl Steinmetz, born in Germany in 1865, had to flee his native country in 1889 because he had joined a socialist club. He arrived in New York City with a cold and little else. "When I landed at Castle Garden, from the steerage of a French liner, I had ten dollars and no job, and could speak no English." U.S. Customs inspectors looked at the 24-year-old hunchback, barely over four feet tall, and wanted to deport him. But a friend convinced the agents Steinmetz was a wealthy and important scientist.

Steinmetz stayed on to become the genius of the General Electric Company, which built him a laboratory in Schnectady, New York. He patented over 200 inventions, discovered laws of magnetism and electricity and became the first person to create lightning in a laboratory. He never gave up his interest in radical ideas and was one of many exiles who stayed in the United States. ■

By 1914, "Madame Walker," as she called herself, had invested in real estate and built herself lavish homes, in Harlem and Westchester County, New York. She also donated some money to the NAACP, YMCAs, and for college scholarships for African American women.

Walker and her staff said they did more than provide unique products. They taught millions of people of color about "cleanliness and loveliness." When she died in 1919, Walker's will left funds to advance the education of Africans and African Americans.

All immigrant success stories were not always so pleasant. Those who became wealthy often found themselves arrayed against other immigrants with little money and less luck.

Born in Scotland in 1835, Andrew Carnegie sailed to America at age 13. He first worked in a cotton factory for $2 a week and bought some property. Then oil was discovered on his land. Carnegie entered the steel production business and decided to dominate the industry by buying coalfields, iron mills, railroads, and sales outlets. He also destroyed his competitors. By 1880, he was one of the richest people in America.

To manage his Homestead mill, which employed 3,800 men from many different nations, Carnegie picked Henry Frick, the wealthy son of a Swiss immigrant. Carnegie and Frick decided to smash the newly formed Amalgamated Association of Iron and Steel Workers that had enrolled 750 workers at the Homestead plant.

Carnegie went on a European vacation, and Frick took over this task. Frick announced a 22 percent cut in wages and, before the union could react, shut down the factory and built a 12-foot-high, 3-mile-long fence around the plant. Then he hired the Pinkerton Detectives to guard the fence and scabs to replace his employees.

The employees were determined to hold their jobs. They had armed patrols circle the mill's perimeter day and night. Other patrols searched arriving ferries and trains looking for scabs.

Then, on July 5, 1892, trouble exploded. Frick had hired 300 armed Pinkertons at $5 a day per man to rush through the picket lines. The men sailed from Pittsburgh to Homestead on the Monongahela River in two barges and were met by 10,000 armed strikers and sympathizers. Both sides opened fire, and the Pinkertons were finally forced to surrender.

The 1892 Homestead Strike pitted a few wealthy immigrants in management against poor, overworked immigrants trying to form the first union in the steel industry. There was violence, and the union was crushed.

The governor ordered out the state militia. Union leaders were arrested for murder, and 160 strikers were tried for treason and lesser crimes. No one was found guilty because public sympathy had swung away from the managers to the workers.

The union then ran out of funds to feed the locked-out families, and the state government continued to intervene on behalf of Frick. Finally the workers gave up.

In 1900 Carnegie and Frick formed the U.S. Steel Corporation, America's first billion-dollar company. The two men continued to make millions, and they donated a fortune to museums, libraries, and colleges. Carnegie and Frick proved the American dream had room at the top for immigrants. But their war against the workers at Homestead also demonstrated that they cared little for those on the lowest rungs of the economic ladder.

C H A P T E R   2 0

THE JOURNALISTS

For immigrants packed into cities, newspapers were a way to preserve the language, hear about the old country, and learn the ways of America. America's ethnic press was also a force to promote nationalist or charitable projects in the ancestral homeland, and self-help, patriotism, and democracy in America. Journalism also began to attract talented immigrants, women, and minorities who made outstanding reputations.

Thomas Nast, born in Germany in 1840, was destined to become the most

Hundreds of foreign language newspapers were issued at the turn of the century.

important political cartoonist of the 19th century. His father, a musician in a Bavarian regiment, made sure his family discussed liberal, secular, and progressive ideas at dinner. In 1846 the Nast family embarked for America.

At age 15, Thomas Nast became an illustrator. During the Civil War, Nast's pictures and cartoons in *Harper's Weekly* stirred the nation. President Lincoln praised his "enthusiasm and patriotism" and called him "our best recruiting sergeant." After the war, Union veterans honored him with the title "artist of the people."

Nast then trained his artist's brush on Boss Tweed, whose corrupt Tammany Hall club dominated New York City government and stole millions of dollars. To dramatize how his city was being eaten alive by Tweed's crooked politicians, Nast created a ferocious Tammany tiger. Tweed angrily told Nast's editor,

> I don't care a straw for your newspaper articles, my constituents don't know how to read. But they can't help seeing them damned pictures.

A Nast cartoon of Boss Tweed.

Nast also created the popular images of Santa Claus, the Democratic donkey, and the Republican elephant. But mainly, he was the artist whose cartoons put Boss Tweed and other corrupt politicians in jail.

Narciso Gonzales was born to Cuban immigrants in 1858, and at age 18 he became a journalist in Charleston, South Carolina. At age 33, he owned his own newspaper, *The State*, which he used to denounce child labor and lynchings of African Americans, and to advocate women's suffrage. These views won him few white friends in South Carolina. Gonzales also exposed Benjamin Tillman, a dishonest politician, who campaigned for office by attacking people of color.

Tillman was defeated in a race for governor in 1902 and blamed Gonzales's stinging editorials in *The State*. One day he confronted Gonzales on a street and fatally shot him. The crime had many witnesses and took place in broad daylight, but Tillman was acquitted by an all-white jury. Gonzales will always be remembered as a man who lost his life in the battle for truth and against racial bigotry.

Jacob Riis, born in Denmark in 1849, was a wide-eyed youth of 21 when he arrived at Castle Garden. When he became a police reporter for the *New York Tribune*, Riis walked the grimy streets of slum neighborhoods to probe oppressive living and working conditions. Sometimes he brought along his camera to record the faces of poverty, pathos, and hope that he saw.

In 1890 Riis wrote *How the Other Half Lives* to provide the public with a look at an urban poverty that lived down the street and around the corner from affluence. *How the Other Half Lives* gained the journalist an important ally, political reformer Teddy Roosevelt.

The politician and the writer teamed up to urge urban reform. Riis also took part in efforts to expand playgrounds and parks.

In 1856 T. Thomas Fortune was born in slavery in Florida to parents whose ancestors were African, Native American, and Irish. He later attended Howard University and worked on the *People's Advocate*, an African American paper. By 1884, he was the new owner of the *New York Freeman*, which he renamed *The Age*.

Fortune's powerful editorials on racism in *The Age* made it the country's leading African American paper. Though some whites criticized him for being radical, Fortune was a Republican even if he was often defiantly independent of the party. In the 1890s he began

Two Dialect Writers

Paul Lawrence Dunbar, born in Dayton, Ohio, in 1872 to former slaves, was the only African American in his high school. But he became editor of the student paper and wrote the class song.

Unable to afford college, Dunbar became a $4 a week elevator operator. He began to write standard and dialect poems, and the latter suddenly brought him fame.

By age 24, Dunbar had published three books of verses. He lectured abroad in England in 1897 and returned to Washington, D.C., as an assistant in the Library of Congress. He helped raise money for black colleges such as Hampton and Tuskegee.

Dunbar's health began to fail in 1899. He contracted tuberculosis. But instead of slowing down, he became even more productive and wrote four novels. Most of Dunbar's writing was nonpolitical, but a few poems and his last novel, *The Sport of the Gods*, tackled bigotry. He died in 1906 at 34.

Peter Finley Dunne, born in Chicago to Irish immigrants in 1867, also made his name writing dialect tales. His fictional character "Mr. Dooley," perched on a bar stool, in an Irish brogue offered simple political wisdom through a brilliant wit.

During a time of rising immigration, labor strife, and political corruption, Dunne's column struck an American note of gentle humor and expressed tolerance for minorities. He jabbed at war, persecution, corporate greed, and phony politicians, and exposed them to the public with a laugh. ■

Paul Lawrence Dunbar

Editor T. Thomas Fortune

T. Thomas Fortune

to write for the popular *New York Sun*.

During the 1890s Fortune helped found civil rights organizations. He also objected to the United States gaining colonies since this would mean white American control over peoples of color in distant islands.

By 1900, Fortune had become the country's most well-known African American radical. He also managed to remain an ally and advisor to the conservative black leader, Booker T. Washington.

In 1923, Fortune became the editor of *Negro World*, the popular weekly issued by Marcus Garvey and his Universal Negro Improvement Association. One scholar has called Fortune "the best journalist the Negro race has produced."

CHAPTER 21

WOMEN LEAD THE FIGHT FOR REFORM

Women in the late 19th century, except in the few western states where they could vote, were denied much of a role in the governing process. Nonetheless, educated and middle-class women saw themselves as a morally uplifting force and went on to be reformers.

Jane Addams was an outstanding example of this new breed of reformer. Shocked by the poverty among Chicago's many immigrants, she opened the social settlement of Hull House in 1889. It offered an array of services to help the poor deal with slum housing, disease, crowding, joblessness, infant mortality, and environmental hazards. For women who held jobs, Hull House ran a day-care center and a boardinghouse.

Jane Addams was only one of many early reformers to take up social work. Jane Porter Barrett, an African American, founded the Locust Street Social Settlement in Hampton, Virginia, in 1890. Her settlement offered black women vital instruction in child care and in the skills of a being a homemaker.

In New York City a daughter of Jewish immigrants, Lillian Wald, began a visiting-nurse service to reach those too poor to pay for doctors and hospitals. Her Henry Street Settlement offered a host of vital services for immigrants and the poor. In 1912 Wald suggested the formation of a Federal Children's Bureau.

By the end of the 19th century, many women reformers focused on the need for state laws

A visiting nurse from the Henry Street Settlement House travels across roofs to visit poor people in their city apartments.

to restrict child labor. Young children from poor families had to work long hours in mines and mills and were exploited by plant managers. No state laws prevented the children from being overworked or abused.

One of the first to challenge the exploitation of orphaned or dependent children was Sophie Loeb, a Jewish immigrant from Russia. After her father's death, she witnessed the desperation of her mother as the family slipped into poverty. As a journalist, Loeb campaigned for widow's pensions when this was still a new idea.

Helen Stuart Campbell, born in 1839 in New York, began her public career as an author of children's books. Then she used novels to expose slum life's damaging effect on women. In 1886 she wrote a novel about two women, one middle class the other a laborer, who break from their dependence on men and chart new lives. In 1891, in *Darkness and Daylight: or Lights and Shadows of New York Life and Women Wage Earners*, she wrote about how easy it was for women's lives to be ruined by poverty and despair.

Lucy Parsons in 1905 advocated use of nonviolent resistance that was later used by civil rights and antiwar protesters in the 1960s.

Florence Kelley, born into a rich Quaker family in 1859, graduated from Cornell University in 1882 and then attended Zurich University. In 1891 she took a job with Jane Addams at Hull House, became an investigator for the Illinois Bureau of Labor, and then was appointed the U.S. Commissioner of Labor. In 1893 she saw that the 8-hour law for working women and children was enforced.

In 1898 Kelley returned to New York City to begin three decades of work at Lillian Wald's Henry Street Settlement. She became a leading lobbyist for minimum wage laws, helped create the U.S. Children's Bureau, and in 1921 secured passage of the Infant and Maternity Protection Act.

Some women went beyond advocating reform to promoting revolution. Lucy Parsons devoted her life to improving the condition of working men and women. Born a slave in Texas in 1853, Lucy's family was a mixture of African, Mexican, and Native American. After the Civil War, she married Albert Parsons, a white man who edited the *Waco Spectator*, a paper that challenged Ku Klux Klan violence in Texas.

In 1872 Lucy and Albert Parsons moved to Chicago and helped to organize labor unions. Albert was fired from his printer's job for speaking in favor of the 1877 railroad strikers. In 1885 Lucy led a march of immigrant families to Prairie Avenue where they protested the greed of the wealthy by ringing their doorbells.

In May 1886, Albert and seven immigrant leaders were arrested for the Haymarket bombing and found guilty. Albert was executed. But Lucy Parsons continued to agitate for workers' rights on picket lines, often with her children, and in articles and speeches. In 1892 she edited a paper, *Freedom*, that denounced lynchings and the sharecropping system that oppressed poor Southerners.

In 1905 Parsons attended the founding convention of the Industrial Workers of the World (IWW), where she urged workers not to go out on strike but to stay inside factories and "tie up the means of production." Until her death in 1943, Lucy Parsons remained a radical voice in America.

To many Americans, Emma Goldman was Public Enemy No. 1. She was blamed for having a part in the attempted assassination of Henry Frick during the Homestead Strike of 1892 and for encouraging the assassination of President William McKinley in 1901. She was innocent of both charges, but she was an anarchist who believed in no government, and she advocated violence toward the rich. In 1893 she was jailed for "inciting a riot" during a hunger strike.

Born in 1869 in Lithuania to a Russian-Jewish family, Goldman came to the U.S. as a teenager. The violence against labor unions turned her from a Rochester factory laborer into a dedicated anarchist. A witty and provocative speaker, Goldman had a lot to say. Since she was often arrested or denied speaking permits, she did not always say all she had on her mind, so she also published a monthly magazine, *Mother Earth*, and wrote two books of essays.

Emma Goldman, feared by many people as an anarchist, was also an early advocate of women's rights and their independence.

Goldman attracted attention from intellectuals who admired her spirit but rejected her anarchist views. She felt that women who only wanted the vote were too conservative. In 1916 she spent two weeks in jail for advocating birth control. She remained an anarchist until her death in 1940.

In 1862 Ida B. Wells was the first of eight children born to former Mississippi slaves of Native American and African ancestry. After attending Holly Springs High School, she began teaching school in rural Mississippi at age 14.

Wells was prepared to pay the price of defiance. She refused to accept southern segregation laws and in 1887 carried a desegregation suit to the Tennessee Supreme Court, where she lost her case. Under the pen name of "Iola," she wrote articles exposing the inferior schools that had been provided for African American pupils by the city of Memphis, Tennessee. As a result school board members fired her as a teacher.

In January 1892, Wells bought a half-interest in a paper called the *Memphis Free Speech*. By March, she was using its pages to expose the lynching of three young African American men she knew. Though they had been accused of raping three white women, she revealed that their white business competitors had planned their murder and had concocted the charge of rape as a justification.

Ida B. Wells was a fearless journalist and speaker who dared to challenge lynchers.

Wells's articles urged her people to resist discrimination by boycotting the segregated streetcars in Memphis or migrating to the West. By this time, Wells walked to work each day carrying two revolvers for protection.

In May 1872, while Wells was out of town, a mob destroyed her *Free Speech* press. Far from discouraged, she decided to launch her life's work — an antilynching campaign. In 1893 and 1894 she visited England to organize international opinion against lynching. One clergyman reported that not since *Uncle Tom's Cabin* had the British been so aroused by an issue and speaker.

An attractive, dynamic speaker, Wells reached thousands with her call for justice. She relied on documentations to prove that the charge of rape was used as a smoke screen to justify lynching. She wrote pamphlets in 1892 and 1895 that used white sources to prove that Blacks were lynched not for rape but for "offenses" such as challenging segregation, talking back to whites who insulted them, or "being uppity."

Her first two pamphlets carried introductions by the famous African American statesman Frederick Douglass. He said, "Brave

woman! You have done your people and mine a service which can neither be weighed nor measured."

After rioters and police rampaged through African American neighborhoods in 1900 in New Orleans, Wells wrote *Mob Rule in New Orleans* to chronicle the white violence. She hoped that when America's "conscience wakes and speaks out in thunder tones, as it must, it will need facts to use as a weapon against injustice, barbarism, and wrong."

Wells took a prominent role in efforts to enroll black women in their own clubs and fellowship leagues. She became a secretary of the National Afro-American Council, and she and other radicals challenged Booker T. Washington for his conservative views. Wells also chaired the Anti-Lynching League and in 1909 she was among the founders of the National Association for the Advancement of Colored People (NAACP).

In addition, Wells was an advocate of women's suffrage and founded the first African American women's suffrage club. In 1913 she served as co-chair of a delegation to President Woodrow Wilson that protested his segregation of the civil service.

More than anyone else, Wells exposed lynchings as a crime against humanity. Her 40 years of unrelenting effort failed to stop the crime and did not produce a federal antilynching law. However, lynchings decreased by 80 percent after her campaign began, and her documented evidence on the crime of lynching and her commitment to justice roused the world's conscience. By the time Ida B. Wells died in 1931, other women and men had picked up her torch.

This African American beauty parade in Bonham, Texas, in 1911 is a demonstration of a modern slogan, "Black is Beautiful."

FURTHER READING

Adamic, Louis. *A Nation of Nations*. New York: Harper, 1944.

———. *From Many Lands*. New York: Harper, 1940.

*The Ethnic Chronology Serie*s. Dobbs Ferry, NY: Oceana Publications, 1972-1990.

Evans, Sara M. *Born for Liberty: A History of Women in America*. New York: Macmillan, 1989.

Franklin, John Hope. *From Slavery to Freedom: A History of Negro Americans*, rev. ed. New York: Alfred A. Knopf, 1988.

Handlin, Oscar. *The Uprooted; The Epic Story of the Great Migrations that Made the American People*. New York: Grosset & Dunlap, 1951.

Howe, Irving. *World of Our Fathers*. New York: Harcourt Brace Jovanovich, 1976.

The *In America* Series. Minneapolis, MN: Lerner Publications, 1971-1990.

Johns, Stephanie Bernado. *The Ethnic Almanac*. Garden City, New York: Doubleday, 1981.

Millstein, Beth and Jeanne Bodin, eds. *We, The American Women: A Documentary History*, New York: Ozer Publishing, 1977.

Moquin, Wayne, ed. *A Documentary History of the Mexican Americans*. New York: Praeger, 1972.

Seller, Maxine S. *To Seek America: A History of Ethnic Life in the United States*. Englewood, NJ: Ozer Publishing, 1977.

Seller, Maxine S., ed. *Immigrant Women*. Philadelphia: Temple University Press, 1981.

Takaki, Ronald. *Strangers from a Different Shore: A History of Asian Americans*. New York: Penguin Books, 1990.

Thernstrom, Stephan, ed. *Harvard Encyclopedia of American Ethnic Groups*. Cambridge, MA: Belknap Press, 1980.

Weisberger, Bernard A. *The American Heritage History of the American People*. New York: American Heritage, 1971.